Great Coaching and Your Bottom Line

Great Coaching and Your Bottom Line

How Good Coaching Leads to Superior Business Performance

Marijan Hizak

BEP BUSINESS EXPERT PRESS

Great Coaching and Your Bottom Line: How Good Coaching Leads to Superior Business Performance

First published in 2019 by
Business Expert Press, LLC
222 East 46th Street, New York, NY 10017
www.businessexpertpress.com

ISBN-13: 978-1-94897-613-8 (paperback)
ISBN-13: 978-1-94897-614-5 (e-book)

Business Expert Press Sports and Entertainment Management and Marketing Collection

Collection ISSN: 2333-8644 (print)
Collection ISSN: 2333-8652 (electronic)

Cover and interior design by Exeter Premedia Services Private Ltd., Chennai, India

First edition: 2019

10 9 8 7 6 5 4 3 2 1

Printed in the United States of America.

Sport has become a world language, a common denominator that breaks down all the walls, all the barriers. It is a worldwide industry whose practices can have widespread impact. Most of all, it is a powerful tool for progress and for development.

—Ban Ki-Moon, UN Secretary-General 2007–2016

(www.un.org,2011)

Abstract

Being a sports coach who is able to contribute to the better business performance of his or her sports organization today is a big challenge. No matter whether it is about amateur, recreational, or professional clubs. Coaches no longer represent some marginal educational resource but are a significant source of new values for sports organizations. They are one of the key factors in the business and sports success of sports organizations. Not only the competitive success, but also the business success of sports organization depends on them.

It is commonly believed that, in order to achieve success in coaching, it is very important to be a good teacher and a pedagogue, and to master in theory and practice technical knowledge about technique, tactics, and conditioning. The aforementioned is no longer sufficient to achieve a successful coach's career, and thus for the successful running of the club. Why? Because today the knowledge of communication and marketing skills is as important as the expertise and the sports results of the coach. Today a coach, along with professional knowledge and results achieved on the pitch, must know how to communicate and must have a positive image. Better sports coaching brings better business results. Although the business success of sports organizations is commonly associated with professional sports, this doesn't mean that business success is not present in amateur sport as well. It is only differently manifested. It is not manifested exclusively through financial but more through promotional effects, such as the positive image of schools, colleges, universities and sports organizations. And even in amateur sport today the matter of persons leading and coaching athletes becomes more and more important. There is growing concern about their abilities, knowledge, and skills that proved to be of crucial importance for the successful running of sports organizations.

Keywords

Sports coaching and business performance; Sports business; Sports management; Sports marketing; Sports coach; Communication in sports; Successful coach; Successful sports organization

Contents

Preface

Sport is not just victories and defeats, athletes and judges, stadiums and halls. Sport is also a business activity. The top managers of sports organizations manage them in the same way as the largest companies are being managed. Everyone familiar with sports structure is aware that a sports coach represents a key factor in a sports success, not only in the competitive success but also in the business success of a sports organization.

This book focuses on the position of the coach, one of the key factors in the contemporary sports industry. The book consists of six chapters. In the first introductory part of the book, general topics about sport as one of the fastest growing segments of the global economy (Plunkett 2013) are discussed, followed by influence of coaching in overall business performance of a sports organization, then marketing as a philosophy that changed the sport, and importance of communication as one of the key factors of the success in the sport.

The fifth chapter of the book is an overview of my views and advice on the role of the coach gathered through quite a few years of working in the professional clubs. The fifth chapter also answers the question "why are some coaches more successful than others?"

It is a common opinion that in order to achieve success in the coaching profession, it is very important to be a good teacher and pedagogue, and to have technical knowledge about technique, tactics, and conditioning gained through education and in practice. The aforementioned is no longer sufficient to achieve a successful sports career as a coach and thus for the successful running of the club. Why? Because today mastering the knowledge of communication and marketing skills as an expertise is equally important for achieving top results in sports. Today, the coach, along with professional knowledge and sports results achieved, must be able to communicate efficiently and must have a recognizable image built.

Although the business success of sports organizations is mostly associated with professional sports, this does not mean that business success doesn't matter in amateur sport. It is only manifested differently. It is not exclusively manifested through financial aspects, but it's more reflected through promotional effects, such as the positive image of schools, colleges, universities, and sports organizations. So the role of people leading and training athletes is becoming more and more important in amateur sport as well. There is growing concern about finding the people with adequate knowledge and skills, as they are becoming of crucial importance for the successful running of sports organizations.

As a former soccer player and marketing director of a professional European soccer club, I've spent my whole career around top-quality sports coaches, talking and exchanging experiences and ideas. Quite a part of what I've learned from these experiences I've put down in this book.

One of the purposes of this book is to encourage you to start investing in your personal development. It will help you to recognize the importance of marketing and communication, the two important issues that will for sure have a positive impact on your personal development, as well as your future business success. I hope I managed to plant the seed of the growing importance of coaching profession in the business success of sports organization in this book. Likewise, I do hope that this seed will soon germinate in the head of a sports enthusiast who would scientifically research and prove its meaning.

The book is written in a simple and easy-to-understand language for everyday use. The style of writing has no scientific character. Regardless of the leisurely style in the book, all my opinions and statements are followed by scientific researches and other books dealing with similar content. I'm confident you'll read it in "one sitting." Please note the fact that the concept of the coach in the book is presented only through a male as the coach (I wasn't lucky enough to have met a female coach), but it also applies, of course, to female coaches!

CHAPTER 1

Sports Industry—Heading to the Top of the Most Profitable Business Sectors

There is a huge amount of money circulating in the sports industry today. Every day we read in newspapers, visual media as well as on social networks about salaries, bonuses, sponsorship deals, and transfers worth tens of millions of dollars in sport. This sounds appealing but you have to be aware that today's sport is subject to constant change because it has to compete for a part of money people are ready to spend for fun and entertainment. And the offer is getting bigger and more complex every day. Sport differs from consumer goods or services because it involves people, and people are inconsistent and unpredictable. This is also the reason why sport itself is attractive, no matter whether you want to be involved in it, participate in its organization, management, or just want to be a side observer.

Across the globe, there is a growing association of sports and entertainment industries. Thanks to the challenges of social networks that increasingly shape the way we spend our leisure time, the sports and entertainment industry records continuous revenue growth. At the same time, sponsorships and media rights appear as the main engines of this growth, pushing the traditional domination of ticket revenue to the rear.

Sports Industry Continues to be One of the Largest and Fastest Growing Industries in the United States and the World

The world at the beginning of the third millennium is not like the one it was 50 years ago. The area of life in which this is particularly manifested is sport. Sport has entered through the small door into all pores of our lives, making it an important part of it—from entertainment, culture, health to the economy.

The sports industry continues to be one of the largest and fastest growing industries in the United States and the world (Plunkett 2013). Sport as an industry is characterized by huge sums of money involved in it today. Big figures sound tempting but they are just a small part of the sports industry. Today's sport is subject to constant changes because it has to compete in a market for the part of the money that has been spent for fun and entertainment. And the choice is every day getting bigger and more complicated.

Thanks to the challenges of social networks that influence our leisure preferences, the sports and entertainment industry has also witnessed a steady growth in revenue. The close convergence of sports and entertainment industry is rapidly growing. At the same time, sponsorship and media rights emerge as the main generators of sport's growth, putting traditional revenue generation into a second plan. The popularity of sports organizations and events is growing every year. This comes as the result of their top organization and marketing exploitation supported by high-tech digital technology that provides better coverage than ever before. Media companies use social media to establish direct contact with sports enthusiasts. Today, most marketing campaigns are already in the very beginning planned as an interaction between the brand and its fans. As an indispensable part of any sports story, the sponsors are also directly related to sports organizations and sports fans. The economic transformation of professional sports has taken a huge leap in the last decade. Large professional sports organizations today are a complex and profitable business. The way in which sports organizations or interested parties respond to the ever-increasing economic transformation of sport raises the discussions all around the world on daily basis. Discussions are mostly held about unobstructed market access including issues such as revenue sharing, focusing on business goals such as profit, shareholder value, and market share.

Just like any business, generating revenue is a constant preoccupation for leaders of professional sports organizations. Unlike companies in other branches of industry, the need to generate revenue in sports is not primarily driven by profit efforts, but rather by the desire to improve sports performance. Bigger revenues allow sports organizations to hire better coaches and players, and improve sports facilities and infrastructure.

The main determinant of generating revenue in sports is the value of entertainment. All sports pay close attention to their viewers, but some sports have a mass appeal because they are passionately followed by people who are not directly involved in sports events. It gives the sport an additional global dimension that attracts media and social networks and results in a level of spending that exceeds far the actual number of participants.

One of the most important factors contributing to the growth of sports in the business sphere was television, in particular satellite television, both in terms of the amount paid for broadcasting rights and the radical changes in the distribution of income among sports organizations.

Although in sports today the professional sports organizations and their athletes and coaches are the ones mostly followed, it would be unjust not to mention the importance of amateur sport. Every year hundreds of millions of athletes around the world enjoy the satisfaction of amateur-level competition. Sport provides many opportunities for professional athletes, but without the driving force of amateurs and amateur athletes who will never become professionals there wouldn't be the top professional sport either. Likewise, without sports stars, professional models, it would be difficult to engage so many children in sports activities. This is the true value of sport: a character built through participation and experience and awards for participation in the team. These lessons often serve as a guide and platform for athletes' success in the real world. Those who are able to apply what they've learned in sports to real life situations can quickly progress in their work. There is a little difference in renunciation that differentiates success in sports from success in real life.

North America and Europe Are Fundamentally Different in Terms of Organizing Sport

As an European and an author who is writing about sports for the American publisher, I want to clarify at the beginning, for the sake of further better understanding of the text, that there is a significant difference between American and European sports. Understanding some of the texts in the book will surely be easier if you recognize this difference since my knowledge comes from an European context.

Although North American culture is largely derived from the culture of immigrants from Europe, North America and Europe are fundamentally different in terms of organizing sport. The biggest difference that sports fans on both continents can immediately notice is the appreciation of the popularity of sports. In North America football, baseball, basketball, hockey, and soccer are the most popular sports. In Europe, the popularity of soccer is far bigger than other sports. Soccer is the undisputed king of European sports, and the popularity of other sports differs from country to country. In Ireland where I live, along soccer the most popular sports are Gaelic football, rugby football, and hurling. In neighboring England, along with the most popular soccer, the favorites are rugby football, field hockey, and cricket. In the eastern part of Europe it is something different. In Russia, after soccer, the most popular sports are ice hockey, handball, basketball, boxing, volleyball, auto racing, athletics, tennis, wrestling, and gymnastics.

What's the Difference Between European and North American Sports?

The European model of sports organization is characterized by two basic features: the system structure of the pyramid and the system of promotion and relegation (Nafziger 2008).

The system of the pyramid structure, as its name suggests, is built on the pyramid as its basis. At the bottom of the pyramid there are sports organizations forming the base. The next level is made up of regional alliances, and sports organizations are members of regional alliances. The next, now somewhat narrowed pyramid level is made up of national alliances whose members are regional alliances. The national alliances level is followed by the level of the European federation. It is made up of national alliances. At the very top of the pyramid there is the World federation consisting of members of the federation of all continents. The cycle of the competition moves from the bottom of the pyramid and the sports organizations, depending on their performance, can climb to the top.

The rise to the top of the pyramid is possible thanks to another key feature of the European model of sport: system of promotion and relegation (Nafziger 2008). Under this system, the worst performing sports organizations in the competition move to a lower division, and the most successful go to a higher division to replace the worst sports organizations in higher-level divisions. In practice it looks pretty simple, because the league formats are very simple. For example, in soccer the winning team gets 3 points, 1 point for the draw, and 0 points for the loss of the game. The team with the most points becomes the champion and together with other two or three teams (depending on the rules of the competition) goes to a higher level of competition, and the team (or two or three teams, again depending on the rules of the competition) with the least score drops to a lower level of competition. Due to its openness, the European model of organization is known as the "open league" system (Nafziger 2008). Open leagues gives to all teams, on any geographic area of a country, the theoretical opportunity to reach the top division and play with top clubs.

Unlike European sports, the North American sports is facing more business side and as such it is treated more like a job done by professionals. It is understandable therefore that the vast majority of Americans can hardly understand the functioning of "open league" since such a system does not exist in North America. In North America there is a system of "closed leagues." This is a system where promotion and relegation does not exist because the number of clubs in the major professional sports leagues of North America (NFL, MLB, NBA, MLS, and HNL) is determined based on the franchise obtained and it does not change. It is constant, and no team drops out of it.

The North American sports system, in comparison to the European, promotes higher equality and competition among the teams, and this makes the great competitive advantage. Equality and competition are encouraged by ensuring a balance between teams through carefully elaborated rules. One of those rules is the salary cap, which limits the amount of money that clubs can spend on wages.

Another important rule is to evenly allocate the highest talents within the league's team (so called draft). It means that the lowest ranked team in the previous season gets the first choice of talented young players who get the right to play in the league next season.

In the closed leagues, the clubs in the competition system and their investors have assurance that they will always be a part of the league (provided they meet certain criteria). Closed leagues in some ways ensure the long-term stability of clubs because they can, with quite a certainty, estimate the ratio of future budget revenue and expenditures, which is very difficult in Europe. The biggest deficiency of closed leagues is that they are limited by the number of places in the competition system. Teams outside the league cannot enter the league based on the sport performance.

There are also big differences between European and North American sports in the ownership of sports organizations and the ownership of competitive leagues.

In most European leagues, it is well known that the clubs do not have the right of ownership of the leagues. Under the influence of American sport, and the fact there are more and more American owners of European sports teams, this has been changing slowly lately. An example of such changes is the English Premier League (EPL). EPL is a corporation made up of 20 teams involved in the league in which the club members act as shareholders. Given the European system of promotion and relegation in the EPL, the league system is expected to change every year, consequently changing the ownership structure of the league each year.

In the North American sports system, the club owners / franchise owners are also the league owners, so there is a clean private ownership structure. The owners have the exclusive right to decide who is involved and to appoint a "commissioner" who has the full power to make decisions regarding the league (essentially a CEO).

Unlike the North American sports system, where the clubs are privately owned "franchises," in privately owned European professional clubs, there is a mixed model of club ownership. There are private clubs in Europe, but there are also a large number of clubs that are public institutions in the community, the so-called associations. Here are some examples of the different ownership structure of the biggest European clubs: Manchester United (England) is a privately owned soccer club (the owner is Glazer family, USA; uk.businessinsider.com 2017). The big Spanish football clubs, Barcelona and Real Madrid, have a specific social ownership model where the fans are the club's owners. The most famous German football club, Bayern Munich, has a mixed ownership model:

75 percent is owned by fans and 25 percent by private investors. Such ownership structure is not a coincidence. In the German Football League (Deutsche Fussball-Liga), there is a rule 50 + 1. It is an informal term used to refer to the clause in the regulations of the German Football League. The 50 + 1 rule states that no single person or entity may hold more than 49 percent of the voting rights in a German club's professional football division (Bundesliga), preventing the sale of a majority stake to external investors, thus protecting clubs from irresponsible owners and maintaining the democratic nature of fan-owned German clubs (www.dfl.de).

When it comes to amateur sport in North America, there is a dominant educational and commercial sport system. The North American amateur sports system is a system in which schools, colleges, universities and commercially managed sports centers form the main principle of organizing sport participation. Volunteer clubs and public authorities have a negligible impact on the system compared to the European system. In Europe, the predominant system of voluntary sports clubs and associations prevails. In most European countries, volunteer sports organizations are actively supported by the public sector, while the impact of business community and education system is negligible.

Is It More Cost-Effective to Invest in Sports in North America or in Europe?

In today's uncertain economic times, investors are looking for stability and predictability. When considering the investment, there are two main things to consider: risk and potential earnings. The higher the risk of investment, the lower the value to invest as fewer people will be willing to accept that risk.

Investing in a North American club is certainly less risky than investing in a European club. Why? Unlike European clubs, North American clubs do not depend on sports scores. Sports results in North America do not have decisive significance on their finances. In North America, a club is at the same time a shareholder of the league, and as such has the power to protect its interests from new participants. In favor of investors investing in North America, there is a regulation of wages, so called salary cap, which gives a guarantee that there will be no large oscillations in the payroll. The risk of investment in the North American club is low and therefore the value of the franchise is very high.

The nightmare chasing the investors who want to invest in the European clubs are unpredictable sports results. If the club has a risk of falling out of the league or not qualifying for one of the continental contests, there is a great deal of uncertainty about future revenue. For the European club to be confident in achieving its profitability through competitive goals, significant financial resources have to be invested in bringing quality players and top coaches. Since there are no regulated rules in Europe that limit the amount of money that clubs can spend on salaries (salary cap), there is an objective risk of inflationary expenditures. The inflation of expenditures is particularly visible at European professional football clubs, which have been taken over by Chinese, Arab, and Russian billionaires. As a result of their takeover, inflation has increased in terms of spending and paying players. Therefore, the FIFA President Gianni Infantino is increasingly thinking of introducing the American model of regulation in commercial and sporting conditions (www.espn.com 2018).

Unlike North America, in Europe (except the English EPL) the investor is not the owner of the league who can easily protect the investments.

Despite all the existing problems, the value of professional sports teams has exploded over the past decade thanks largely to the massive increases in television rights fees paid for the games.

Investing in sports clubs and affiliated auxiliary companies that roll billions of dollars in sports business in North America and Europe is, despite existing risks, an attractive and profitable business. High consumer demand, power, price, and media demand are key to success and big sports teams and leagues bring with them greater financial benefits. The fact that sport is a great and profitable business is best shown through the entry of the big Internet business, Amazon, in sports business. Amazon bought part of the TV rights for matches and summaries of the EPL (the English Premier League) for the UK region from 2019 to 2022. Amazon will offer the matches on Boxing Day and 20 more games over the week through its streaming service Prime (www.bbc.com 2018).

Certainly in sports, besides the benefits, there are always risks that can spoil the "good" investment. We must never forget that sports business is primarily affected by emotions. The same human or emotional factors that make us today to spend our last dollars on sport product can equally prevent us tomorrow from doing so because of unforeseen events.

There Is a Growing Need for Skilled Sports Staff

Along with the growth of the sports industry, there is a growing need for staff educated to deal with the unique nature of the sports industry. With increasing employment opportunities in the sports industry, there is also a growing need to educate sports experts. Educational institutions around the world have quickly adapted to the growth of sports activities and have developed a large number of curricula and programs at the graduate and undergraduate level to meet the need for specialists trained specifically in sports management (Stier 1993).

The accelerated growth and popularity of sports have fueled the constant desire of many people to continue their career in the sports industry. A large number of students every year, both in the United States and abroad, are enrolling in academic sports programs to prepare for their future career in the sport business. A large number of them, among other programs, choose sport programs to become coaches.

The increase in demand for sports is due to its strong development and social media exposure in the past twenty years. The increasing trend of professionalization in sports reinforces the demands for coaches and other professional staff in sports. Behind the increased demands, there is often a disparity between high expectations of the public and difficult conditions in which athletes, coaches, and other professional staff are working. Professionals in professional sports are increasingly struggling to cope with the high expectations of the public.

Working in sports industry is not an easy job. The sports industry is subject to a high level of public oversight. Thanks to social networks, coaches, athletes, and sports management are evaluated by sports fans and parents, I can emphatically say, on a daily basis. Since most estimates of sports enthusiasts and parents are influenced by emotions, it is clear that they do not give credibility to the people who make the assessment. But public expectations are high and members of sports organizations must be aware of them and must know how to deal with them.

Sport Stars

Sport stars are an integral part of today's sport. They are a personalized expression of top sports values. Without them there is no real spectacle or spectators. Sport stars are not only a source of income, but also an indicator of the effectiveness of a sports organization or sport event. Because of the interest of sports enthusiasts, appearances on social networks, and the attention of public magazines, the participation of sports stars gives a special charm and quality to the sporting organization and competition they are participating in. Stars, because of their successes and popularity are able to attract the attention of the whole sporting public to the sport they are engaged in and to the sporting organization they are performing for. They are able to inspire a multitude of young people to enter the world of active sports and also pull thousands of spectators to watch them. It is not exaggerated to point out that the entire marketing system of top-notch sports is based on sport stars. This is also the basic economic explanation of their astronomical income.

According to *Forbes* magazine (2018), the 100 best-paid athletes made in the period from June 1, 2017 through June 1, 2018 a total of $3.8 billion, including endorsements, which is 23 percent up from the previous year. Their earnings include salaries, bonuses, prize money, endorsements, licensing, and appearance fees.

On the list of top earners is Floyd Mayweather ($285 million, boxing, U.S.) followed by Lionel Messi ($111 million, soccer, Argentina), Cristiano Ronaldo ($108 million, soccer, Portugal), Conor McGregor ($99 million, MMA, Ireland), Neymar ($90 million, soccer, Brazil), LeBron James ($85.5 million, basketball, U.S.), Roger Federer ($77.2 million, tennis, Switzerland), Stephen Curry ($76.9 million, baskeball, U.S.), Matt Ryan ($67.3 million, football, U.S.) (*Forbes* 2018).

The earnings of sport stars are provoking excitement among moralists, who are forgetting that the top scholars and other professionals, such as attorneys, actors, singers, politicians, businessmen, also charge for their media popularity.

Obviously, as shown by the list of their earnings, sport stars are a grateful promotional marketing tool. The high income earned by sport stars is an acknowledgment for their talent, work, and dedication. Behind their earnings there is the global popularity and recognizability of their status. Sport stars are authentic because they are visible, understandable, and their value can be checked. Unlike the effort of some athletes to try to gain the status of an athletic star by violating regulations, various privileges, unfounded publicity, or support of the potentate with no talent and effort. The sports public cannot be deceived because before or after the shabby glow of such fake "stars" comes out.

Public Spending on Sports Infrastructure and Organization of Major Sports Events

There are few things that can unify the world. One of the phenomena that has this power is a big sports competition. The Olympics and the FIFA World Cup are a unique example of events that have the power to unite people of all colors and religion in the interest of sport.

You probably wonder how come I did not mention the Super Bowl (NFL), the biggest celebration of American sports? I did not mention it because events like the Super Bowl (NFL) or World Series (MLB), the Finals (NBA), the Stanley Cup Finals (NHL), the MLS Cup Finals, unlike the Olympic Games and the FIFA World Cup in football, primarily aim to unite the inhabitants of North America.

North America and Europe, apart from different approaches to organizing and valuating of sports, also differ in the organization of major sports events. In North America, sports are part of the city's strategy and are largely based on investment in the infrastructure (stadiums) for the needs of national professional teams. Over the last decade, American cities have offered professional teams great incentives, such as the construction of new stadiums, to make them relocate from their domicile cities. In Europe, something like this is unthinkable.

In Europe, cities and states are more focused on hosting great sports events, such as World or European Championships in various sports: soccer, athletics, basketball, handball, volleyball, tennis, rugby, and boxing.

As with all sports events so are the mega-sport events subject to schedule and the country in which they are held. In practice, there are positive but also negative examples of economic justification of the organization itself. Particularly encouraging and positive is the strong indication that

sporting events have been shown as catalysts for the economic development of cities and host countries in terms of international tourism spending (www.visa.com).

Countries and cities are organizing large sports events for a variety
of reasons, including branding, building the necessary infrastructure,
and economic development. Unrealistic expectations of the city or state's
economic development following the organization of sporting events are
often subject to discussion by economic experts.

In 2006, Professor of Economics at the College of the Holy Cross,
Victor A. Matheson, in the research "Mega-Events: The Impact of the
World's Largest Sporting Events on Local, Regional and National Econo-
mies" came to the following conclusion:

> Public spending on sports infrastructure and the organization of
> large sports events necessarily entails reducing costs for other pub-
> lic services, increasing government borrowing or increasing taxes,
> and all this represent a burden to the economy. At its best, public
> spending on sports facilities has a null net effect on the economy,
> as the benefits of higher employment are undermined by the neg-
> ative effects of higher taxes and lower spending in other segments
> of public services.

Matheson also argues that when assessing the economic effects of large
sports events, the significant costs of security and alignment of "general
infrastructure" with "sports infrastructure" are often ignored (Matheson
2006).

Unlike analytical economy experts, sports event organizers, sports
organizations, and professional team owners are bent upon trying to stress
on the great economic impacts from events to justify heavy public subsi-
dies. I am convinced that the interest in organizing mega sports events in
the future will not disappear, but it is certain that the costs of infrastructure will be rationalized, especially if after the completion of mega events
it does no longer serve purpose.

In the past, most sports facilities were single-purposed, which means
that neither more purposeful use of facilities was considered nor the
effectiveness of future management. Today, there isn't almost a single

community that can afford to maintain a single-purpose facility. In addition to its multifunctional use, it is of crucial importance that the manager of the facility, in search of efficiency and effectiveness possesses knowledge of factors that can contribute to its successful operation.

Such an example of building the necessary infrastructure is the bob competition at the Winter Olympics, which after competition is finished no longer serves the purpose and is deteriorating shows that it is necessary to carry out rationalization of infrastructure investments. This is just one of example of irrational investment, and there are for sure much more. The reflection of such an International Olympic Committee policy is that fewer and fewer countries are interested in organizing the Olympic Games.

CHAPTER 2

Better Sports Coaching Delivers Better Business Performance

Behind every successful athlete, team, or sports organization there is a high-quality coach or a team of managers. There is growing concern about their skills and knowledge, which are of crucial importance for the successful running of sports organizations. An organization system is increasingly being established in which the management of the club, including the coach, is subject to daily learning. It is a new pattern of behavior that represents a big universal change in the traditional culture of sports management. A sports coach does not represent a marginal educational resource of the club any more but is a significant source of new value for the club. Today, it is not simple to become a leader and coach of the new "Z" generation of athletes who check every move or word on Google, and at the same time are difficult at acknowledging authority. The sports organizations that achieve top results, whether professional or amateur, are the ones who have discovered how to open the way to the new ideas and different abilities of people at all organizational levels.

Behind Every Athlete There Is Always a Coach

There are many different individual roles in the sport that have found their place in the books. In this book the central role is dedicated to the role of a sports coach.

Behind every athlete there is always a coach. There is no sports program aiming to achieve high-quality performances or to change behavior of players without the full participation of the coach. The coaching role is not static, and it is constantly expanding and amending. It does not only include aspects directly related to sport, but also psychological and pedagogic ones, all in order to cope with the growing demands of modern games and athletes. It is already well known that coaching profession is no longer exclusively tied to sports arenas and athletes solely. The area of activity and responsibility of coaches has been expanded to communication with parents, taking care about athletes' health, their training and education. In professional clubs, the coach's role has been further expanded and includes communication with media, sponsors, administrative team management, nutrition, transfer and player contracts, club promotion, and determining the structure of the club.

Along with the organizational tasks and oversight of technical, tactical, and physical aspects, the aforementioned duties of the coach can be compared to the function of CEO (chief executive officer) of the company because it includes responsibilities that go far beyond mere knowledge in the field of sports education. It is a difficult and complex profession, but also exciting and extremely diverse respecting the educational and creative activities it involves.

Summing up the coach's responsibilities it is no accident that his abilities, knowledge, and skills are increasingly questioned, as they are becoming crucial for the successful running of sports organizations. Sports organizations are increasingly establishing a system of organizations in which management, including coaching, is subject to everyday learning. It is a new pattern of behavior that represents a major change in the traditional culture of sports management. A sports coach's role no longer represents a marginal educational resource, but it has become a significant source of new value for sports organizations. As already mentioned, the new "Z" generation of athletes is very demanding as they are checking everything online. So in order to achieve top results, the sports organizations have to be wide open to new ideas and abilities of people at all organizational levels. Have you ever asked the person you just met what he or she is doing or what is his or her occupation?

The first thing that goes through my mind after I find out what's the person's occupation is whether that person is competent for that job. This is an important thing for me, because in a profession where you deal with people, such as managers in the business, teachers, doctors, and of course coaches, professional qualities are not the only ones that matter. Social virtues are highly required. Coaches must know how to communicate! It is no longer sufficient to rely on purely technical-professional qualities because the success of a coach depends on how good he is getting alone with athletes at the social interaction level, how he talks to them, how he directs and inspires them in order to achieve common goals so he can actually "lead."

The entertainment scene across the world is increasingly accepting new heroes. Athletes are the heroes of the new age. They are sitting in the same line with until-recent inviolable singers and actors. Thanks to their global popularity, sports organizations have more sponsors, viewers, and social network followers, more jerseys have been sold and all of these bring money in. In glorifying athletes people often forget that underneath their success lies the painstaking work directed by a coach. The only way to maximize the talent of an athlete is to fit it into a system of training and playing. This process isn't possible without leadership and knowledge.

The role of a coach in forming of an athlete is precious. Sports coaches besides being leaders are often the role models who move forward athletes, sports organizations, and sometimes the entire community. For this reason, coaches play a multifaceted role in athletes' lives. It is a role that reaches beyond the teaching of the principle of sport.

The development of the society, and the sport environment (rich athletes, demanding employers, fans, media, and sponsors) has influenced the fact that the profession of a sports coach today can be with certainty characterized as one the most demanding professions in the world. Through applying positive learning experiences, the coaches, apart from maximizing athlete's potential in sports and life, can highly contribute to the business success of sports organizations.

The coaching profession is a really tough job that requires special and versatile people. In training, there are many elements of pedagogy, and this is especially obvious when introducing new activities. For this reason, it is necessary to create a positive environment for learning and efficient transfer of information. In a positive environment, it is easier to learn and influence those who are trained. The dream of each coach is to enable athletes, his students, to reach the maximum level of their ability. This is not easy to achieve. In order to succeed, the coach must understand the needs and abilities of athletes, their moods, and their fears. And when he understands all of it, still it is not enough; furthermore, their respect must be necessarily gained.

It is no surprise, therefore, that in sports every day the role of the people leading athletes is becoming more and more important. Successful sports organizations, either professional or amateur, are only those who have discovered ways to open the doors to the ideas and abilities of people at all organizational levels.

Whether you want to admit it or not, most of the sports organizations, including those in college, are primarily focused on achieving results. This is somehow understandable, because sports results generate various benefits for a sports organization. Based on success, benefits can be manifested through various forms, ranging from increased application to the university to better financial performance of a professional team.

It is well known that students often choose a school, college, or university based on the recognition of their sports teams. The general recognition and image of educational institutions is largely created by the media, through its thorough monitoring of school itself and student competitions.

There are a large number of scientific studies that have confirmed the impact of sports success on student applications. One such study is the "Impact of College Sports Success on the Quantity and Quality of Student Applications." Devin G. Pope and Jaren C. Pope have elaborated a comprehensive set of data on school applications, SAT scores, control variables, and sports performance indicators. Their data set consists of all (about 330) NCAA Division and schools from 1982 to 2002. Based on the processed data, they have proven that football and basketball success by college teams can have a significant impact on the number of applications the school receives (ranging from 2 to 15 percent depending on the sport, success rate, and type of school), and modest impacts on average quality of students, measured by SAT scores (Pope and Pope 2009).

Educational institutions are definitely aware that the success of their sports teams, especially in football and basketball, attracts students and generates donations. Sport is undoubtedly one of the tools that can directly affect the reputation and prominence of educational institutions.

The influence on the reputation of an educational institution is perhaps best shown by the data from last year's (2018) College Football

Playoff National Championship. In the College Football Playoff National Championship Final at the Mercedes-Benz Stadium in Atlanta, Alabama defeated Georgia in front of 77,430 spectators. The event was telecast live by the ESPN sports channel (collegefootballplayoff.com).

How many future applications and donations will this great success bring to both teams, given the top-level media coverage of the event?

Do Coaches Contribute to the Business Performance of a Sports Organization?

Thanks to the many years of working in sports, I had the chance to convince myself that a quality of coaching staff can significantly contribute to the business performance of the sport organization. Let me give you two examples which I am familiar with.

Highly trained and talented athletes have always had a very good position in the sports market. In Croatia (Europe) where I have been working in sports, a large number of professional sports clubs can thank their financial endurance for many years now solely to selling of their best players. Croatian professional sports clubs are simply forced to sell their best athletes, mostly overseas, because in a small and market-uninteresting Croatia with the population of only 4 million, it is difficult to close the financial circle. Thanks to the continual creation and sale of athletes and coaches, Croatia is now recognized as an exporter of talent in the world of sports. Revenues that come from sales to Croatian sports clubs are not negligible. I will list only some of the today's most famous athletes whose transfers significantly contributed to Croatian Club budgets: Saric (NBA, Minnesota Timberwolves), Bogdanovic (NBA, Indiana Pacers), Ivica Zubac (NBA, Los Angeles Lakers), Ante Zizic (NBA, Cleveland Cavaliers), Modric (soccer, Real Madrid FC), Kovacic (soccer, Chelsea FC), Lovren (soccer, Liverpool FC), and Mandzukic (soccer, Juventus FC).

In the 2018 FIFA World Cup (soccer) in Russia, Croatia emerged as the runners-up, which has brought global popularity to Croatia and increased the market value of Croatian players and coaches on the world football market.

It is evident that the players mentioned had to be "created," since the talent solely is not enough to reach the top athlete's level and play in the NBA or one of the most crowned European football clubs like Real Madrid. There are many coaches working on development of Croatian athletes, and the cycle of sports education lasts for at least eight years. All of them are credited with the fact that their clubs earn significant financial resources each year through the transfer of players.

Another example of the impact of the coach on the business performance of a sports organization will be closer and more comprehensible to readers from North America. It is linked to the work of one of the best-known coaches in the National Football League (NFL)—Bill Belichick, the Head Coach of New England Patriots, who is of Croatian heritage. In the football world, coach Belichick is known for recognizing talent and having the ability to draw out the best of his players who are playing in unusual positions and unconventional formations. Thanks to Bill Belichick, Patriots have maintained a high level of game play for many years, with no overly big and expensive stars. In addition to the excellent results that have contributed significantly to the business performance of Patriots' success, he is also known for being keen to help players to increase their own abilities followed by increase of their value on the market. Patriots' performance is most evident in the continued creation of top players at the highest level. Not only Belichick creates top players, but also motivates players from other teams to come to his club for a lower contract, which also contributes to Patriots' business success. One of them is Deion Branch, who in 2002 signed a five-year, $2.93 million "low" contract with Patriots. In cooperation with Belichick, Branch soon became a major name for the NFL. Only four years later, in 2006, the Patriots sold Branch well to Seattle Seahawks. Branch signed a six-year contract with Seattle Seahawks for $39 million and a $13 million bonus (Groysberg and Naik 2016).

The difference in the value addition created by Branch at Patriots thanks to Belichick is just one example that shows a big influence of the coach in sports organization's business performance.

Among the academic researches proving that high-quality coaches can improve the performance of sports organizations, I've chosen to mention Lawrence Kahn's study –"Managerial Quality, Team Success and Individual Player Performance in Major League Baseball" published in *Industrial and Labor Relations Review*. In 1993, Lawrence Kahn analyzed the data from the Major League Baseball from the period 1969 to 1987 to assess the impact of the quality of manager on the team and on the performance of individual players. Utilizing the winning percentage of the team in a given year as a dependent variable, managerial quality, percentage of earnings over the past year, and additional controls, he empirically demonstrated that manager's ability was a very important factor in transforming the players' performance into victory for the baseball team (Groysberg and Naik 2016).

Kahn further found, through additional analysis, that big coaches help players to achieve their full potential. His extra analysis has shown that great coaches help players achieve a better individual performance. He empirically documented the influence of a new high-quality coach. Kahn believes newcomers may have a positive impact on the team if they are better than their predecessors. With the arrival of a better coach, the average player's performance in the season is improved. The high-quality coaches have deployed their players by placing them in situations where they have the greatest chances of success (Groysberg and Naik 2016).

Thus it can be concluded that the teams employing quality coaches increase both team and individual performance of sports organizations. By these findings, Kahn confirms that recruiting quality coaches is crucial both for the organization and for individuals. Bill Belichick's performance in Patriots is a good example.

The cost-effectiveness of creating players in Croatia, Belichick's work scope, and the results of Lawrence Kahn's scientific analysis are three valuable examples that support my effort to present the importance of the role of a coach for successful business performance of a sports organization.

What Can We Learn from a Sports Coach?

The role of a sports coach is quite similar to the role of a manager in corporate business and as such can be mirrored to the leadership role in corporate business. In the business world the most difficult issue is to implement the team spirit and the atmosphere that sports coaches are able to create in their teams. Tommy Lasorda, head coach of the Los Angeles Dodgers for 20 years, said: "My responsibility is to get 25 guys playing for the name on the front of their shirts and not the one on the back" (cmoe.com).

As Tommy Lasorda has explained in a picturesque way, corporate business managers should strive to ensure that all business team members act in the interest of the company rather than in the personal interest. Success in sports and business is solely team work and not individual. In sports the players on the pitch must constantly communicate, adapt to each other, and change their approach to meet the demands of the game. They are interdependent, helping each other, communicating all the time. They do not expect the head coach to make all decisions. The coach is just one of them. The coach is the one who motivates team members to help each other on the pitch. A corporate business could be regenerated through a number of sports values. Bringing a quality coach to a sports organization means making progress. Likewise, hiring a quality manager in the company positively affects employees and business operations.

The example of a player coming to Dallas Patriot with an effort to increase his value, as I've already described, can be compared to the corporate world. There are many examples of employees willing to accept the job for a lower starting salary with the same goal. Large corporations such as Apple, Google, Amazon, and Microsoft, often use their positive image as a source of competitive advantage to attract, exploit, and retain gifted employees at lower costs to the company.

I've read an interesting story about the implementation of the Dallas Patriot leadership structure and philosophy in the Subaru dealership business on Portland Road in Saco, Maine. The owner of the company, Adam Arens, thanks to the tireless work inspired by NFL football coach Bill Belichick, created a sales team with happy employees entitled to full medical benefits, profit-sharing system, financial management, and strong employee relationship.

"There is a Kraft-Brady-Belichick model from which we draw," said owner Adam Arens. "It's the longevity of pairing. The longer you stay with your wife, the longer we work with our co-workers and our employees and clients, the better we are for each other. It's a must, but the beauty of their three there, they have different roles and responsibilities" (www.nfl.com).

There is really something to learn from Dallas Patriots. They are not necessarily the best as individuals. Most of them do not represent top or elite players. But they are incredibly fast in adaptability. When the environment changes very quickly, it is not only about the one who is powerful, but about the one who is agile. Changes in business are as fast as in football, so there is definitely something we can learn from sports.

Leadership Off the Pitch

Being a sports coach today is a big challenge. The challenge is to have the opportunity to share your potential and part of yourself with the generations of sports enthusiasts, regardless of whether they are amateurs or professionals. The profession of a coach, if approached responsibly, meticulously, and ambitiously is extremely demanding.

Due to the coach's interaction with various stakeholders (i.e., players, auxiliary staff, media, supporters), his role can also be considered the most important position in a professional sports organization (Ogbonna and Harris 2014). The position of the head team coach in professional sports organizations can be compared to the position of leading executives in companies.

Due to constant sports development, the coach's obligations are increasingly transmitted to areas outside the sports field every day. The scope of off-field commitments is particularly noticeable in professional sports. Most of the existing professional sports researches are focused on field leadership, coaching, or game behavior, without recognizing the role of various interactions with key nonfield players that can highly contribute to leadership roles.

There is only a small number of studies where the importance of leadership behavior outside the context of coaching are emphasized. One of these studies is "Leadership Off the Pitch: The Role of the Manager in Semi-professional Football"(Molan, Matthews, and Arnold 2016). The Irish authors have explored the role of coaches outside the sports field, using semiprofessional football in Ireland as a base for their research. The participants in the survey were four coaches of the first team, four players, and three board members of the semiprofessional football clubs in the Irish League. Six key leadership topics were identified regarding the role of managers with off-field players. These are: team vision, performance expectations, behavioral expectations, effective communication, individual consideration, and the use of archetypes. The study also identified leadership topics in relation to coach's role with other key stakeholders including cooperation with management, leadership through auxiliary staff, and influence on the media.

The authors predict that the results of the study will encourage coaches, football clubs, and national associations to put more emphasis on education on the leadership skills that are required from coaches (Researchportal.bath.ac.uk).

Intelligence Plus Character Make a Great Coach!

The title of this text is a paraphrase of the wonderful thought of Martin Luther King Jr. who said, "Intelligence plus character—that's the goal of true education" (www.schreyerinstitute.psu.edu).

Why is intelligence one of the main prerequisites for the success in a coaching job?

Intelligence, simplified, is the ability to adapt to different circumstances. How does intelligence manifest itself in a coaching practice? There is, for example, Matthew Stafford (Detroit Lions) who is a star player. Can you approach Matthew in a similar way you approach Jake Rudock (Detroit Lions) who is just an "ordinary" team player? You have to find a way and if you are not intelligent, you simply cannot cope with that challenge.

My experience of working with four top Croatian soccer coaches (Miroslav Blazevic, Branko Ivankovic, Zlatko Dalic, and Drazen Besek) confirms that along the expertise and intelligence character is an essential assumption to become an excellent coach. Thanks to working with them I realized that an excellent coach possesses not only the aforementioned attributes but also possesses distinct personality character traits. Possessing character traits like perseverance, self-awareness, credibility, fairness, and self-control makes the difference between good and excellent coaches. The coach's character traits are "inexhaustible" and are hardly noticeable in the first impression. They come to express themselves in time and cannot be copied or imitated.

Perseverance is one of these remarkable traits that every excellent coach possesses. Persistent coach does not avoid problems but is willingly exposed to risks and temptations to develop persistence. The new generation of coaches are not endowed with patience and that is somehow understandable. We live in times of rapid, instant success, and thus persistence is not easy to develop. Persistent coaches are not being obsessed to make a top career at 45 years of age, they do not cheat, do not complain constantly, and they do not give up. They believe in their knowledge and they are sure their work and knowledge will eventually pay off. The importance of perseverance is very well described in an excellent book titled *Grit* by the well-known psychologist Angela Duckworth.

Self-consciousness is the characteristic that manifests itself mostly in knowing and accepting our own "weak points." What everyone else sees, but to us, it is hidden and unknown. To be able to manage players successfully, you need to know yourself. How to find out which are your weak points? Ask your associates, friends, those who know you best. Do not expect an answer from the players, or those who need you, because you will not receive accurate information from them. The most valuable information you will get from the ones you least agree to.

You may not be aware that you are talking a lot and listening poorly. You may not notice that you are talking one thing and doing the other. In revealing your weak points, you do not have to expect that you will hear negative things only. You may also find some good, beautiful things that will enhance your self-esteem. The top coaches are aware of their weaknesses but also of their strengths. Get to know your strengths and weaknesses. Only coaches who understand that are able to build their own motivation, personality, and tendency to the environment that helps maintain credibility.

You must have often heard of a certain coach that he has been credible. What does that mean? This means that when he says something, he stands behind it, even though it is in opposition to the trends or the opinion of the majority. Credibility is when you act the way you say. During my work at the professional club, I often encountered different instances of coach's inconsistencies. The most common were situations when coaches made rules that have been later violated by themselves because they haven't been applied equally to all players—players "stars" were excluded and privileged.

I've seen, too, a lot of cases when coaches talk to players about smoking hazards and unhealthy food, even though they were passionate smokers themselves and eating unhealthy food. Normally, the players did not take them seriously.

Only when we talk about things from our deep beliefs that we adhere to and practice, we can have an impact on the players. The players are wise and smart, and they notice and follow everything you say and do. They will forgive you when you sometimes lose your nerves. They will forgive you forgetfulness, laxity when dressing, but if you talk about one thing and do the other at the same time, you will not have authority over the players. LA Galaxy forward, Zlatan Ibrahimovic, is known not only for his skills but also for his statements where he generally praises his own "character and works." Do you think he is baffled and arrogant about what he is saying? You probably don't, and that's because he's a sincere, authentic, and brilliant example of accepting himself. He is credible, no matter what you think of him.

Righteousness is the next coach's virtue, which means treat others the way you want to be treated. Fair-minded coaches play by the rules and do not take advantage of others. As a coach, you need to learn and to model what fair play is about. Make sure you are reasonable and you treat everyone equal when making decisions. Always think about the feelings of all people, which will be influenced by your actions and decisions, and so treat all players based on impartiality.

You have to have a great memory in order to become a righteous coach. I do not talk about the memory of a guy who came to the club for the first time. I'm talking about the kind of memory I had when I was a player and I've been coached myself. The things I liked and disliked about my coach. So, it's about remembering how your coach motivated you and how he also de-motivated you. Many lose that memory. They became coaches themselves, so they forgot. They start acting like a boss, bossing around, and if you have a good memory, you'll understand. Perhaps some player's behavior is unacceptable and you will let him know it, but you will also understand why he made a mistake.

Self-control is, according to my choice, the last important element of coach's personality. Self-control is indispensable in training, leading games, and teaching children, but also in relationships with parents, judges, and officials. We often witness that coaches are unable to control their emotions when it comes to players and judges' mistakes. I am aware that for me it is easier to write about it than for coaches to handle it when faced with injustice or when things are happening against them.

A coach who cannot control his emotions, a coach who screams and jumps creates an atmosphere that does not contribute to learning and entertainment nor to the spectators' satisfaction.

Practice skills that enable self-control. You will surely become a more satisfied and successful coach.

The Successful Coach Who "Digs the Most Gold"

A football coach is nothing more than a manager in a gold mine. Don't get me wrong here—gold in this metaphor represents the players. A successful coach is one who digs the most gold, which always has to be of high quality to meet the demands of the media, the public, the sporting public, and sponsors. To achieve this, it's simply not enough to be just a "leader" of the miners. He must be a visionary and a strategist. Someone who will determine the ways and means to bring the miners to the "gold." Maybe you'll find my comparison with a gold mine ridiculous. After extensively following Irish and Croatian coaches, this gives me every right to say that this is correct. The strongest confirmation of this claim of mine is backed up by watching the paths of football players who have reached their peak under the leadership of Croatian coaches such as Miroslav Blazevic and Branko Ivankovic. These players today represent the future of Croatian football. Players such as Suker, Boban, Modric, Mandzukic, and Kovacic represent a mere fraction of the great players whose careers were led by Blazevic and Ivankovic. In carrying out the coaching, the "mining work," a lot of coaches have been helped by the fact they are thorough and meticulous, studious and professional. This is why it's extremely important that the coach is a team player. To be clear, the team must always know who has the final word. The coach must, after taking over the team, establish quality two-way communication with his colleagues and players. He must present his vision of achieving the set goals so the members of his team can easily put it into practice. And they must never underestimate their status. The coach is the leader of the team. He is the moving spirit. His role is most important in terms of synergy. Soccer is not a fool's game as some may think. Soccer is a mind game, where it's just not enough to run fast but also be a quick thinker. The heart of the tactics set by the coach is the off-the-ball movement, the speed of receiving the ball, open play, and so on. When working with players, apart from the technique, tactics, and physical conditioning, as a coach you have to take into account the psychological, social, and cultural environment of the team. You need to trust your players and associates by actively involving them in your work. Sadly, the sporting public doesn't value "coach miners" enough. Today the sport is dominated exclusively by the desire for successful results. You've either got it—or you haven't. If you've got it, you're successful. If you haven't, then it's time to pack your bags. I think the competition result by no means should be the only measurement of the quality of a coach's work. True coaches should be valued according to the "gold" they dig!

To Be Successful You Must Be Different from Others

It is often said that a coach is a man who knows on Friday what will happen on Saturday, and on Sunday he explains why it did not happen on Saturday. A profession of the coach is no longer linked to the pitch, individual, or the team exclusively. Today, along with the work on the technical and tactical fields, a coach must communicate with the media, sponsors, and fans but also show to players by his example how to behave, look, and represent themselves in their environment. Knowledge of communication and marketing skills can help any coach because don't forget that the mere fact that someone is a good coach is not a guarantee of his or her success. This is telling us that sports coaches must work on their improvement constantly. Knowledge is a prerequisite for success in any business and especially in a profession that involves working with people.

Fortunately, the time has come when there is an increase in demand for high-quality, educated coaches with a positive image. Although they are not "cheap," they do not have any problems in finding a job. You could also become one of them. By investing in your knowledge, you are indirectly investing in your image. Although there is no major difference in creating the positive image of athletes and positive image of coaches, there are some specifics in creating the image of a coach. Today in order to become successful in any field of action, you have to be distinguished from others. Quality verbal and nonverbal communication is a prerequisite to creating a positive image.

The Very Fact that Someone is a Good Coach Is No Longer a Guarantee of His or Her Success

I suppose you might be one of those wondering sometimes why are some coaches more successful than others, although they have, for example, the same level of knowledge or abilities.

Why are they better "sold" on the football market, how come they are moving without any problems from small to more reputable clubs, constantly advancing and achieving financial and status benefits?

Why do the media like to interview and quote them, and players like to train with them more than with others?

What is it that distinguishes them from their colleagues?

Someone might think that they are charismatic, someone will add they follow modern sports trends more than others, and that they have more feelings for players. Someone might even think they have better contacts or know some influential people. There could be a part of the truth in all these answers. A comprehensive explanation that applies to all such coaches, regardless of their personality or communication profile, is that to achieve success, it is no longer enough to be just a professionally recognized coach who delivers results.

Today, the coach has to know how to present his knowledge and the results achieved both to his environment and the public. To achieve success in the coaching profession, it is very important to get familiar with communication and marketing skills. Because today the sports public is more or less influenced by marketing communication.

The sports audience, which consists of players, fans, club management, viewers, media, and sponsors, do not evaluate the coach according to his coaching work and results achieved solely. He is also evaluated as a person, according to his communication with the public. The public will remember the sports results of the coach, but the way he presents his personality is crucial for gaining respect or disrespect of the public.

Each coach's appearance is a communication—a message that spreads and creates either positive or negative image.

If you want to build a successful coaching career in sports, you have to master basic communication and marketing skills. If you do not know how to present yourself and your knowledge, it is highly likely there will be no results.

CHAPTER 3

Marketing, A Philosophy that Has Changed the Sport

Thanks to marketing, sport has become one of the largest businesses in the world. Marketing in sports is different from marketing of other ordinary products and services, but most "common" marketing techniques can also be applied in sports.

Using the marketing concept in sport assumes that the key to achieving goals lies in determining the needs and satisfying the wishes of those who use its services. Marketing aims to create as much awareness and loyalty as possible toward the service we make use of. The more it is used in communication, more successful the sports marketing becomes. The marketing concept has revived today's sport and brought it closer to millions of people. It has contributed to the fact that many coaches, athletes, sports clubs, and sponsors see their future in the ability to better understand the users of their services and their importance for better functioning and development of sports.

Finally, in the world of sports and entertainment, everyone is keen on the one who can deliver the most exciting and most credible story. Thanks to marketing, sport regularly delivers exciting stories from College Baseball Home Run Derby, Champions League, Olympic Games to Super Bowl.

All Successful Marketing Programs in the Sport Are Market-Oriented

Philip Kotler, generally considered the father of marketing, has given the following definition of marketing:

1. Marketing is the process by which an organization relates creatively, productively, and profitably to the marketplace.

2. Marketing is the art of creating and satisfying customers at a profit.
3. Marketing is getting the right goods and services to the right people at the right places at the right time at the right price with the right communications and promotion (Kotler 1991).

The customer is in the center of the marketing concept along with delivery of values that will satisfy his or her desires and needs. Sport marketing applies this marketing concept in all subareas of sport. The fundamental aim of sport marketing activities is to meet the buyers' need for products or services that offer benefits better than the ones from competition while at the same time achieving the highest sustainable profit (Sullivan 2004).

All successful marketing programs in the sport are market-oriented, meaning that it is necessary to know what sports fans (those who are engaged in sports, or follow certain sport) want in order to respond to their needs. To be market-oriented in sports means to develop a system of gathering information from competitors and customers of sports goods and services and to include this information in planning and decision making in order to explore competition and develop an appropriate marketing strategy. A well-made marketing strategy will enable us to choose the best way to achieve the goals set.

The aim of sports marketing is to provide the best possible service to the customers and in turn to build as much awareness and loyalty as possible. The more it is approached as a communicating factor, the more successful sports marketing is.

Unlike "classic" marketing, marketing in sports has one additional specificity, and this is a powerful influence of emotions in making a buying decision. Market-oriented sports organizations, athletes, and coaches are committed to sensitizing, serving, and satisfying their fans' needs. They are doing everything needed to ensure high quality and top value for their followers. The marketing concept has revived today's sport and brought it closer to millions of people. It has contributed to the fact that many coaches, athletes, sports clubs, and sponsors plan their future through the ability to better understand the users of their services and their importance for better functioning and development of sports.

Today, in the world of sports and entertainment, it's all about delivering the most exciting and most credible marketing content. Digital media played a major role in the development of sports marketing. Thanks to digital media, marketing content can be tailored to fit different groups and individuals, along with the possibility of direct interaction.

What Are the Main Marketing Goals of Sports Coaches?

A sports coach is one of the key figures in the sport and therefore has to establish quality marketing communication with the environment. In order to succeed, the coach has to define his marketing goals. Once the goals are determined, the process for achieving the goals has to be elaborated in detail (strategy) and ultimately the coach must be consistent in the implementation of this process.

The main marketing communication goals of the coach are:

- presentation of his own professional knowledge and skills (attracting attention);
- highlighting comparative advantages compared to other coaches (creating interests);
- fostering public interest—good positioning among the opinion makers (incentives to purchase);
- achieving the goal (action).

Opinion makers who create public opinion about coaches are media, social networks, sports forums, sponsors, and various sports institutions and organizations. As you can see, the goals of marketing communication of the coach only differ in articulation from the basic postulates of successful marketing communication of commercial products. In order to implement an effective goal management strategy, a coach must communicate in a clear, coherent, and convincing manner. A well-designed and implemented strategy to implement the objectives of the coach ensures progress in the profession. The coach has to fully control and monitor the dimensions of achieving the goals set so that they become recognizable by sympathizers and fans, and the work done is considered as high quality and successful. The marketing communication goals of the coach should be seen as related units whose achievement takes place in such a way that the hierarchy of achieving one goal promotes the achievement of the other, and all in an effort to achieve the marketing effects for the coach as efficiently as possible.

A Winning Combination in Sports: Marketing Mix

It's been a long time since sport was communicated solely by words and pictures. Today the communication takes place through the marketing mix. "Marketing Mix is a set of controlled variables through which a company can influence the customer's response" (Kotler 1991). Marketing mix is one of the dominant ideas in modern marketing and consists of everything that the company can use to increase the demand for its product. The elements of a marketing mix are product, price, place and promotion, and Kotler has called them shortly as 4Ps. All of the above elements are equally important in achieving the marketing goals and work together. These four variables help the company develop a unique sales point as well as a brand image (Kotler, Armstrong, Wong, and Saunders 2008).

Sports Products and Services Are Becoming Recognizable Thanks to Promotion

Modern sport is an integral part of the market orientation of society, and as such it is inconceivable without promotional activities in the process of linking sports goods and services. Promotional activities in sports mean different activities used by sports organizations and companies to target the potential customers with the aim of encouraging them to buy certain goods and services. Thanks to the promotion, sports products and services are becoming recognizable to individuals, groups, or the public, with the aim of creating a positive attitude.

A positive attitude and adequate knowledge of a sports offer is the first step in purchasing products and services of sports organizations.

Coach: The One from a Wide Range of Sports Products

A sports coach is nothing more than just one from a wide range of products in the market. In marketing terms, coaches have been identified as an integral part of the overall sports product (Rosner and Shropshire 2004), as they are considered as an important precondition affecting the overall market efficiency of a sports organization.

Sports organizations have become recognizable not only by the athletes but lately by the coaches as well. Thanks to their frequent presence and huge coverage by the media, their popularity has even outgrown the athletes. Equally as the products differ, the coaches also differ from each other.

The characteristics of a coach that differentiates one from the other are called the coach's personality. Personality refers to individual differences in characteristic patterns of thinking, feeling, and behavior. Studying personality focuses on two broad areas: one is to understand the individual differences in particular personality characteristic, such as sociability or irritability. Another is to understand how different parts of a person come together as a whole (http://apa.org).

Personality is the strongest link that makes a difference between coaches, and also highly influences the creation of their positive image in the public. Spectators and followers of sporting events may be delighted with the results achieved by the coach on the pitch, but only through the way in which his personality is presented, either respect or disrespect is earned.

Respect and appreciation of coaches are of great importance for strengthening the positive image of a sports organization in public. A positive image of coaches in the public almost always gets transfixed to the team that leads (Rosner and Shropshire 2004). In the professional clubs, the public relation departments advise coaches how to behave in the public. They teach them how to become positive, safe, and capable personalities. Additionally, in order to create a positive image, media exposure can be increased, for example, through targeted interviews aimed at highlighting their characteristics and demonstrating the competence of the coach (Ross et al. 2006).

Coaches can also be encouraged to participate in community-related events or to start writing their own columns/blogs to maintain their public visibility and to continue to act as a reminder of their team's names (Mullin and assoc. 1999).

Brand Increases Competitiveness

Brands are more than just names and symbols. Brands represent consumers' perceptions and feelings about product and its performance—everything that the product or service means to consumers. As one branding expert suggests, "Ultimately, brands reside in the minds of consumers" (Kotler+3 2008).

Brand is a tool that increases the competitiveness of sports organizations, athletes, and coaches in the market. Branding serves a dual function. In addition to identifying the source of the customer's product and guaranteeing quality, it also protects the producer from mixing with a competitor selling apparently identical goods (Aaker 1991).

Sports coaches today need an effective brand strategy in order to establish a positive relationship with the environment and across the public and to gain a greater degree of loyalty of the team. Brand in coaching profession can be the decisive difference between the coaches of the same quality level. Given the high competitive nature of sport, branding can play an important role in influencing fans' preferences and club-based perceptions and distinctions from competing clubs and other leisure-time activities (Bauer, Stokburger-Sauer, and Exler 2008).

The strength of a coach who is a brand simplifies the decision-making process, reduces risk, and reflects quality and high expectations. Basketball coach Gregg Charles Popovich is today recognized as a coaching brand in North America, meaning that his coaching value in the sports market is much higher than that of a school team coach. The difference between a "branded" coach and an "ordinary" coach is that brands are not created on the pitch, but in the perception of people.

The most famous brand in the world is Apple (Forbes 2017). The company name represents a certain image and identity, as well as the product itself. What would Apple mean without a name? Just one of the many manufacturers of electronic products, and the cult iPhone just one of a number of mobile devices on the store shelves. The world is full of top coaches today, but clubs mostly engage those who have developed their own identity and image, that is, those who have become a brand. There are no sports fans who have not heard of Bill Belichick, Glenn "Doc" Rivers, Gregg Popovich, Lovie Smith, Jose Mourinho, and Pep Guardiola, as all of them are recognizable brands on the world stage of sports.

Thanks to television, the growing commercial strength of coaches has contributed to the increase of public and club interest for individual coaches as marketing subjects. Top coaches are no longer just coaches, they are also celebrities, sports icons; in a single word, they are brands. Coach brand as a public person strongly influences people's behavior and hence they are engaged by large companies to promote and validate their products. Coaches and their agents came to the position that, because of reaching the "star" status, they are able to negotiate with sponsors about contracts to promote various products (from sports equipment to juices and cars) in order to increase demand for these products. In the sports world there are plenty of examples of top sports coaches who earn far more from sponsorship than what they earn on the soccer field.

In the sports world, there is even the example of Jose Mourinho, the big soccer star, former Manchester United coach (EPL), whose name and signature was protected as a European trademark in 2005 by Chelsea FC. The purpose was to stop various businesses trading with his name, and using his public image without his permission (www.techdirt.com 2016).

Is Quality Essential in Determining Value of a Coach?

Evaluating sports is very difficult and complex. Customers make the decision whether to "buy" a certain sport based on personal imaginative values, friends' opinions, media influence, depending on whether the sport is well covered by media, or well-known because of a sports and media star. Players, coaches, and athletes must always draw the benefit of their participation in relation to the costs. Today, in the sports market, there is a great deal of competition among leisure time activities offered, so it has to be considered how much the costs can negatively affect their participation in the chosen sport. Sports practice shows that when designing a price for a particular sports product, primarily the market circumstances at that particular time have to be considered. Although the belief that for the acceptability of a certain price level, the objective quality of a sports product is essential; in practice, this is only partially correct. Objective quality is just a part of the crucial subjective rating of a potential buyer of a sports product (a spectator, a sports club), which for sure involves the image of a sports product, meaning the opinion created and the customer trust in the sports product.

Even though the public believes the quality of a certain coach is the most important factor to determine his value, again in reality, this is only partially true. The decision of football clubs and associations whether or not to hire a certain coach is made based on personal imaginary values, the opinions of the media, perception of him created by the media, and the results achieved. The price of a coach is negotiated on the basis of his expertise and results, but these aren't decisive for agreeing to the final price. The actual quality is only part of the subjective assessment of the one who is actually hiring. An important component of the judgment is the image of the coach or the public image formed by the respective coach. Actual trends show that price estimation of certain coaches is based primarily on the market conditions at a given moment. The expertise, results, and appropriate license are all considered to be obligatory. In determining the final price, the way in which a coach presents his knowledge and person-ality in public is essential. A coach, who has built a stronger public image, generally achieves a higher market price. What does this mean in practice?

The engagements of former sport stars by famous clubs confirm my opinion. They often get a coach's job on the account of their well-known name, even though there are certainly better and more experienced coaches among their counter-candidates.

My opinion has no scientific and researched background. It is based on my long-standing experience of work in Croatian soccer clubs.

Never Regard Sports Journalists as Enemies

It happens often that the coaches are not happy with the news or article published in the newspaper. Not a reason to despair, as journalists are people just like everyone else, with their strengths and weaknesses. Journalists also have the right to be wrong—it's just that their errors are visibly exposed to the public, unlike others. Many of them have their own pet coaches as well as those they don't particularly respect.

Usually young coaches, at the start of their coaching career, are extremely sensitive to the opinion of other people and media criticism. They might even contact the journalist who wrote a negative article to explain that he or she is wrong. Their pride demands explanations and evidence for the way a particular article had been written. They are not aware that this means adding fuel to the fire. Later on, looking back, these responses may seem amusing. Because of life experience, they realize it's much more important to know how to remain indifferent to criticism than to constantly explain to people that they've been attacked without any basis. The same applies to the relationship with the media. Through experience, they realize that probably more than half of those who bought the paper that day didn't even pay attention to the article that made them so angry. And the question is if those who did actually read it understood the article in the same way it appeared to them. The truth is people don't think so much about others, but mostly themselves. It worries them more not to have taken their dog for a walk than whether the coach of their favorite players made a ludicrous substitution during the match. But you also have to be aware that building trust and respect between coaches and journalists takes a lot of time, effort, hard work, tolerance, and patience.

My advice to coaches would be to meet media representatives in person as it makes cooperation easier. Don't be suspicious of the media. Most journalists are highly committed and take pride in their work. Sport journalists have to be seen as an essential partner in the joint venture. Not as enemies, not even those you've had a bad experience with in the past. You must be aware of the public eye's great interest in sports, as well as coaches. You also have to accept there'll always be someone hoping to criticize your work unfairly. When you take this inevitable fact on board, life gets easier. Keep trying hard, do the best you can, and just smile at the comments, complaints, tiny digs, and criticism. This, by far, is the best recipe. In the past, we can find various examples of different coach behavior toward journalists. In the early 1980s, the coach of the Italian national soccer team, Enzo Bearzot, accepted his players' initiative when they defended themselves from the sly journalistic comments by simply ignoring the media. This is where the accepted notion "Silencio Stampa" was coined—not giving a statement to the press. This wasn't just within Italy as it was later adopted across the world and became a tactic accepted by many coaches. I don't support such an attitude of coaches and athletes toward journalists, because it's counterproductive. Avoiding statements doesn't mean a breakdown in communication, it's just a breakdown in talking with the media. Messages transmitted by silence speak a lot more, but one thing is certain—they don't bring people together.

Coaches on the Rise or Fall:
Never Refuse Journalists

Thanks to television, sport has become a global game and sports coaches have been transformed into celebrities due to their regular TV appearances. We live in an age where coaching careers are increasingly influenced by the media. Although we're told most of coaches only live on results and success, this is only partly the truth. These days, this is no longer enough. Today, a successful coach, along with his professional knowledge and results on the pitch, has to have a certain level of popularity and a personal image. Those who achieve popularity know how to promote their work, which can be done easily through the media. The coach must never forget the importance of the media, even when at a low point and likewise when doing well. The media is represented by journalists who are the link between coaches and the interested public. They're the ones who transmit the coach's thoughts and shape the image of the coach in the public eye. Why do coaches attract the attention of the media? Because they're public figures, and also the audience wants to hear expert feedback on certain moves in the game. Journalists love interesting, witty, and charming interlocutors. Among those who deviate from the stereotype is Jose Mourinho. Not a day goes by without a statement from the "special one", not only for the English, but also other international media.

Journalists prefer easy-to-reach and available coaches. If you avoid the press, if contact with them becomes a burden, and if you're bothered by certain questions and criticism, journalists will eventually avoid you too. Talking of relationships between coaches and journalists, I always think of an interesting remark by a friend of mine, a sports journalist: "he was never refused by a coach who was at the start of his career and equally who had a problem."

He was always refused by the coaches who at some point felt powerful and untouchable, forgetting that the wheel of fortune constantly turns and can one day find themselves back at the bottom. The third thing that attracts reporters is the coach's expertise. Knowledge can fascinate everyone, including journalists. The media is the long arm of the public and the soul of the fans, and that's the way coaches have to experience it. Naturally, the media will sometimes be of harm, but it will also provide a good opportunity for free promotion. It often depends on coach himself and his relationship with the media. It's simple: seize the media!

The Place of a Sports Product Can Significantly Affect the Achievement of Overall Marketing Goals

The place of sporting goods refers to where and how consumers are buying sports goods (in marketing, the concept of distribution is also linked to the sports product). The place in the provision of sports services relates more to the location than to the physical marketing channels (wholesale and retail). The location in the sport represents a marketing space where spectators, contestants, or recreational athletes are gathered. The place of a sports product is an essential element of a marketing mix, since it can significantly affect the achievement of overall marketing goals. This impact is particularly noticeable in competitive sports where it is very important that sporting events are timely and spatially matched to other events so as not to overlap. Very important from the position of the location is availability, that is, traffic connection to the sports arena itself. The place is a particularly important element of marketing mix for athletes and coaches. Can you imagine the situation you got an attractive offer to train a team in central China tomorrow? Suddenly, your future workplace location would become the most important element of a marketing mix. All of this tells us that all elements of marketing mix are equally important and interrelated.

Social Networks: A Huge Step Forward in Sports Marketing

The appearance of television was crucial for moving sports from local to global level. Thanks to television, the sport has widely opened its window to the world. Along with the development of electronic media followed by expansion of new commercial technologies, the sport has become a global good, and the sports industry one of the most profitable global businesses.

The sport today, due to the use of new technologies, is now available in every part of the globe. And where visibility is, there are always sponsors and advertisers who have quickly recognized the marketing value of the sport. The result is the incredible popularity of top-class sports clubs, athletes, and coaches who even, through their frequent appearances in the media and social networks, succeed to put in shadow elusive actors and musicians.

In winning the new markets for sports clubs, the social networks are far most supportive. Reaching, interacting, and communicating with fans through digital and social media are much more effective than traditional television.

Marketing of sports organizations has completely adapted to sports fans with regard to comfort, speed, and price, all thanks to social networks. The marketing in sports itself also has to adapt to the new technological changes. The upgrading, new ways of thinking, and acting are required. If sports organizations want to grow and develop, the existing concept of marketing skills and practices must be constantly refined with new competencies and practices that technological progress brings. Use of social media in sports means a major marketing step forward. Many authors over the years have clarified what social media actually are. Kaplan and Haenlein (2010) define social media as a group of Internet-based applications that build on the ideological and technological foundations of Web 2.0, and that allow the creation and exchange of user-generated content. The content of social media can contain text, audio, video, and networks. Social media are not only used by young and adult people to inform and share their personal images and messages between family and friends. They are used by sporting organizations around the world for the purpose of promotion and interaction with sport fans in a systematic way.

Social networks like Facebook, Twitter, Instagram, Snapchat, and YouTube have become media destinations for sports organizations. Thanks to the interaction with fans on a personal level, their loyalty to the sports organization as well as to the products and services it offers is growing stronger. Social media has also played a major role in the global promotion of sports, which resulted in intensified interest of sponsors to invest in sports. The sponsors have very quickly noticed a great interest in the content of sports on social networks.

The social networks enabled sponsors to build new relationships with fans and sports enthusiasts and their potential consumers, thanks to their mutual point of interest—sports organization, event, player, coach. Mangold and Faulds (2009) also say that social media have become a major factor in influencing different aspects of consumer behavior, including awareness, information gathering, opinions, attitudes, buying behavior, communication, and evaluation after purchase.

Large European sports clubs, which have always been economically inferior to American professional clubs, have expanded their businesses to the whole world through the social networks and thus approached the American clubs on financial indicators. The largest expansions of European clubs happened on the Asian continent. In 2012, the Mailman, the social media agency from China, launched an interesting Red Card China Digital Awards. The award is based on an annual survey that ranks the digital competence of the most popular football clubs, leagues, and players on major Chinese social media platforms: Sina Weibo and WeChat. The Red Card 2018, the award for the most influential team in 2018 on major Chinese media platforms, was won by Manchester United followed by Real Madrid, Bayern FC Munich, Arsenal FC London, and Liverpool FC.

> *With over 107m followers, China is one of Manchester United's most important markets and we have a long history of innovation and fan engagement in the region. Through data analysis, geo-specific content creation and on-the-ground activities, we continue to be the most followed football Club on China's major social media platforms: Sina Weibo and WeChat. We are honoured to receive the Red Card award for the second consecutive year and we are excited about the ongoing opportunities to innovate and build our brand, allowing our fans in China to interact with the Club and our products.*
> —Phil Lynch, CEO of Media, Manchester United
> (www.irishmirror.ie 2018)

German Bundesliga is the number one European football league title online in China. Among the players, Christian Ronaldo, the last year's winner, was replaced this year by Lionel Messi from Barcelona as the most influential player in China (soccerex.com 2018).

Current positions already established in the huge Chinese market point out that during 2019, the integration of new technologies and a wide range of fans inclusion will be the key to success in the sports industry. To capitalize on their popularity financially, sports clubs will have to find ways to get closer to supporters at a deeper level that will increase their club value.

The Top Coaches Are Also Sports Stars, Right?

Due to the great interest of sports enthusiasts and attention drown by media and social network users, top coaches represent a special element of their team's quality. What is it that makes the coaches sport stars? Sport stars are personalized expressions of value. Given that coaches are able to attract the attention of the whole sporting public to the game and the club in which they work, they also deserve to be given the epitome of sport stars. It is therefore understandable that coaches and sport stars are the most suitable subject for promotion and other marketing activities. It is not a surprise that today's entire sports entertainment system is largely based on sport stars. The statement pronounced by stars followed by the interest provoked in the public largely gives an economical explanation of their huge income. Their income is huge because they bring profit both to their sports organizations and to all participants in the sports chain.

Sport stars are worshiped by the public because their results are authentic, visible, understandable, and their value can be checked. Sport stars, along with their popularity, besides motivating young people to engage in sports, also inspire the interest of the general public for a particular sport. Thanks to the wide recognition of their stunts, spectators are attracted to TVs, mobile phones, and sports stadiums, thus contributing to the sports success and financial success of their sport and team. All of these elements have to be taken into account in marketing deliberations of sports.

The Image of a Coach from the Marketing Point of View

Whether they like it or not, sports coaches definitely create a certain image. The question is only whether they create it alone or allow someone else to do it for them. If a coach wants to create his own image, he has to find a way to develop it and to hold onto it, respecting the fact he is constantly under the watchful public eye. This especially applies to the top professional coaches. A positive image created in public is of great significance in achieving the goals set.

Each coach should work on his image. The marketing theory on the concept of image says: "The image is a set of beliefs, ideas and impressions of a person about a particular subject or other person" (Kotler 1989). Following this theoretical definition, the image of the sport coach can be defined as the image he is experienced by the public. This image often differs from the image the coach has on himself. The idea of a coach sometimes can be far bigger (lesser) than the real quality and the sport results he achieves, because the image created in the public is not only based on sports achievements, but also on presence in the media, behavior, looks, and other factors that are not directly connected to sports results.

It does not matter what the coach thinks his value is, it matters what the public thinks his value is. Aren't we witnessing examples from the sport practice when frequent appearances and glorifying a coach in the media resulted in his huge transfer to another club? Each coach has a personality that makes him different from his colleagues. Based on the personality of the coach, either positive or negative attitudes and associations are created by the public concerned as well as coach's environment. (Malovic 2005).

Writing about the image, the leading Croatian media expert Stjepan Malovic noted that "the image is a tool used to communicate and reveal your qualities, competence and abilities to others."

Below are the basic elements of personality elements needed to build a positive image, which can be used by sport coaches as a helpful tool in everyday life:

Appearance—Fans and the public mostly do not have opportunity to meet the coach personally so the judgment on him is based on his appearance.

Communication capability—Fans and the public expect the coach to communicate equally successful as his team and players are led.

Character—A good character is the virtue that everyone admires. It is a result of upbringing, education, and other environmental impacts. Character evolves throughout life.

Body talk—The gestures and movements of the coach should transmit the message of security and self-control in order to gain trust from public.

Attitude—The coach must have his own attitude. He must believe in his value, in the value of his players, and his team. His attitude greatly influences the opinion and the judgment of the players and the public.

Style—Today there is a very high level of competition among coaches, so it is advisable for the coach to develop this unique quality to be more recognizable than his colleagues.

We live in times surrounded by visual stimuli literally at every step. Thus it is impossible to achieve a successful career in any public profession without paying attention to one's visual image. Through further education, or by recognizing the importance of the mentioned elements, the coach can empower his image. Today to be successful, no matter what your profession is, you have to differ from others. This also applies to sports coaches. The quality communication is the skill that to a known extent creates a positive image of a sports coach. The mere fact that a coach is an excellent expert in his profession does not guarantee success if he is the person difficult to cooperate with. Creation of positive personal image needs to be embedded in everything he says and does and it will help him to make a successful career. Critical contacts happen on a daily basis in the work of sports coaches. The coach should constantly be aware of the way his communication with people is, both in public and in private life. A sports coach should also always keep in mind that in the public he is presenting his players and his club (alliance), so he must constantly take care of his communication, even during the match time, which is one of the most stressful moments in the life of a sports coach.

Many times people make assumptions about a coach as a person solely on the basis of his appearance, statements and behavior along the edge of the field. A positive image will bring to every coach a secure corner at the moments when he is the object of negative media attention so the coach needs to carefully choose his statements and behave accordingly. Time is needed to build an image. It is a long-term process that needs to be constantly upgraded with positive assumptions.

The soccer coach Miroslav Ciro Blazevic belongs to one of the most crowned Croatian coaches thanks to his top sports results. Apart from achieving excellent sports results, Miroslav Blazevic is the coach who has managed to build a great coaching image. As I was fortunate enough to cooperate with him for a while (in 2004), I got to know his way of communication and to know how he manages to provoke interest in the media and the public. Thanks to him, there was a growing interest in both the club and its players. Through studying his communication and his opinion of the elements needed to create the positive image of a sports coach, I noted down some of the most important ones:

- **appearance** (the coach must always look neat and clean);
- **communication** etiquette / sport culture (the basis for creating a positive image of each coach);
- **style** (the superior coach must develop his own style);
- **knowledge** (the coach must continually invest in his knowledge because who knows the knowledge does not know about fear);
- **the ability to communicate** (the coach does not need to be a big speaker, but must speak clearly and understandably);
- **good communication with the media** (no large or small, all media are significant);
- **respect for all people** (by respecting all people the positive message is transmitted);
- **authority among the players** (created by knowledge, discipline, honesty and justice);
- **sports achievements** (they confirm and give credibility to the image created).

Thanks to keeping up with these postulates, Miroslav Blazevic managed to communicate with the public in a very good manner, thus complementing the sporting image of one of the best soccer coaches in the world (Drazenovic and Hizak 2005).

CHAPTER 4

Communication: One of the Key Elements for Success in Coaching Profession

Whether the coach speaks or not, he's always communicating! Signals are sent through his appearance, the tone of his voice, gestures, and movements. So it's impossible not to communicate!

When the coach deliberately or unintentionally happens to ignore players, journalists, or fans, again he's communicating messages. Thanks to their communication, the coaches become recognizable, as communication gives them added and unique value that sets them above the rest. Every word, every smile, greeting, and handshake with an athlete or fan is a message that'll be remembered for a long time. Good quality communication is one of the basic requirements of a coaching profession.

Coach as a Person is Being Assessed According to His Communication

To succeed, it's no longer enough to be recognized as a skilled, talented, and result-oriented coach. Today, a coach must know how to present his knowledge and the results achieved to those around him, to the public, and to the whole world. To achieve coaching success, it's important to gain an insight into communication and marketing skills, primarily as today the public interest in sport is under a certain influence of marketing communications. The sporting public, which consists of athletes, fans, club management, spectators, the media, and sponsors don't evaluate a coach exclusively according to his professional work and the results achieved on the pitch; he's also measured as a person, according to his communication with the public. The public will always remember coach's results, but the way his personality is presented determines whether respect or disrespect of the public will be gained. Every appearance is a communication opportunity; a widely spread message creating a positive or negative impact. Among coaches there's a common opinion about the things that mostly matter in achieving success. These are usually to be a strong teacher and educator and an expert in technique, tactics, and the fitness regime, both in theory and in practice. I only partly agree with this opinion. Today, the way a coach presents his personality and his professional work is just as important, if not even more important than his actual expertise and pedagogical quality. A coach can only succeed if he is able to use appropriate communication in order to promote his work and sports achievements. Thanks to the know-how of marketing and communications, a coach can win sympathy and provoke emotions among the sporting public. The more emotions a coach provokes among the public, the stronger his odds of gaining sympathy and, in turn, receiving better coaching job offers. Essentially, if a coach doesn't know how to present himself and his expertise, the results won't follow.

Words or Not, the Coach Always Communicates

A coach communicates, making direct contact with the players and those around him, on a daily basis. Personal contact is of great value to every coach. It opens the door to direct two-way communication with the players, exchanging information, feedback, and everything that promotes positive communication. It's impossible not to communicate! Whether you speak or not, you're always communicating! Signals are sent through your appearance, tone of voice, gestures, and movements.

When you deliberately or unintentionally happen to ignore players, journalists, or fans, again you're communicating messages. Efficient communication gives you added and unique value that sets you above the rest. Every word, every smile, greeting, and handshake with a player or fan is a message that'll be remembered for a long time. Good quality communication is one of the basic requirements of a coaching job. It's extremely important that as a coach you cherish two-way communication with your team so that your goals and vision are shared among all of your players. Communication of the coach exclusively with the captain is simply not enough. You have to communicate with all members of the team so they can later transfer your messages, passion, and enthusiasm to the new-comers in the team. The personal contact of the coach often depends on the attitude of interlocutors before the actual communication. The greater the cultural similarity between the coach and player in terms of origin, education, preferences, and beliefs, the higher chance of successful communication.

Individual talk with players is always a very important aspect. Especially at a time when a player is going through a tough time or not performing well on the pitch. Davor Suker was once a marvelous player who could beat any opponent. But I am sure there were times during his career when he literally wanted to do everything on his own. And this is impossible in soccer. His coach, Miroslav Blazevic, must have got annoyed and displeased with his performance. He would have had to talk with Davor Suker in private. Such individual conversations would have taken Davor Suker a step forward. With his lucidity praised by the coach, he would be thrilled to listen to him and take on board his every constructive criticism. Following each interview, he would be able to regain his motivation, and we would once again see the unstoppable Davor Suker—the fear of the rival's goalkeeper.

Speaking and Listening as Indispensable Tools

We all talk to each other, but not all of us have managed to master the art of high-quality clear expression. Not all of us know how to engage in conversations aiming to resolve, rather than encourage conflict. Without the ability to clearly present what you know and what you want your players to be taught, you won't be able to achieve meaningful communication. You simply won't be understood. The biggest problem of most coaches is they're not aware of what they're saying and the way they come across to their players. The importance of personal exposure is increasingly becoming important and so it's important the coach knows how to communicate well with the public.

For the players to properly understand the coach, his communication must be complete and professional. This can only be achieved if he sends a consciously planned spoken message and afterwards look to receive feedback on its acceptance and effects. The feedback he gets becomes the foundation of relations between coaches and players. Feedback improves the preservation and development of high-quality and effective communication. In order to be understandable to players, the coach has to use clear, understandable language, concise sentences, words that they are familiar with and specific speech. Each coach can improve and upgrade the quality of his communication, thus preventing miscommunication among players. The way to do this is primarily by listening.

Do you sometimes forget the right word when explaining something? This could mean your vocabulary is not wide enough and needs to be broadened and enriched. How can this be achieved? There's no better way to enrich your own vocabulary than reading books. Listening also plays a significant role in reaching a strong level of communication. Not without reason, nature has given us all one tongue and two ears. We should listen twice as much as we talk.

Unfortunately, we don't use this gift of nature as well as we should, not being aware how the quality of our lives could be improved by listening. It's simply impossible for a coach not to communicate. Equally, silence is a powerful tool. On many occasions, silence has more of an impact than any spoken word.

Half-Time Communication?

A break during half-time is a significant moment for the coach. It's an opportunity to draw attention to both the good, but also the negative aspects of the game. Over the last 20 years since I've been around different coaches, I've heard hundreds of stories and different approaches to the players at half-time. I wonder whether it's even possible in such a short time to show players everything that a coach noticed during the first half. So, what exactly is the most effective thing to do for players during a quick 15-minute break? To ensure the coach's messages are useful and effective, first of all they need to be short, simple, and clear. Brevity and concise information is essential as there's very little time available. Players still need an additional few minutes to freshen up, rest their feet and re-energize ready to get back on the pitch. The coach's short comments during half-time should initially provide feedback to the players on their game and instruct them how to resolve problems that have arisen in the game. This can't be done using general phrases, such as "you have to score a goal," "you're not concentrating enough," or "the defense is open." Given the short timeframe, the coach should concentrate on practical advice, in order to give players valuable suggestions to improve. Practical advice can often be connected to the pitch conditions, and can for example, in harsh weather conditions, subtly, and sometimes even drastically, affect the result of a game. If it rains, the surface is slippery and the ball travels faster. Do all players wear suitable boots for such conditions on the pitch? Is it windy? The team that attacks with the wind behind them certainly has an advantage over a team that plays against the wind. What's the pitch like? Is it short, long, narrow, or wide? These are all factors that influence the approach of a certain game and which every coach needs to make his players aware of. Narrow pitches allow pressure inside the penalty area; therefore the defensive players should be warned when the ball is on the bounce. Players should be encouraged to constantly put pressure on the ball as it increases the possibility of an opponent's errors, and in turn increases the chances of gaining higher ball possession. Do players follow the ball and attack opponents as soon as they receive the ball, or wait? Finally, it's always useful to remind players to communicate and talk more with each other. Football is a game where you don't use your hands. But, remember, there aren't any rules prohibiting the use of your voice! Players should be encouraged to use their voices as a resource on the pitch, because communication between the players is an essential tool in defense and attack. "Watch your back!" "One-two!" "Mine!" or "I've got it covered!" During half-time it's not good to only analyze mistakes. It's also very important to emphasize the positives in the game and boost the players' motivation levels. This is something many coaches fail to do. Criticism during half-time is mostly counterproductive, especially when you are losing. A positive approach to communication enhances the confidence of players and increases the likelihood their trained skills will be repeated. The half-time break is the perfect opportunity to emphasize the goals set by the coach. Regardless of how many things the coach has on his mind, he shouldn't talk about everything. He should selectively identify a few key changes that can help improve the game in the second half. Every wise coach will always leave a little time for his players to speak during the break. Players too have a certain perspective on the game, despite the attitude of the coach. Their comments and suggestions can often be useful in addition to the coach's words during the break. Then there are the substitutions. They are a result of how well the coach reads the game and must be used as a useful tool for the coach to improve the play of the team. The course of the game simply cannot be predicted prior to the start of the game.

CHAPTER 5

Why Are Some Coaches More Successful than Others?

Have you ever wondered why certain coaches are more successful than others, even though they may have the same level of knowledge or skills? Why are they more highly valued on the sports market and simply have no trouble moving from small setups to more prestigious clubs? How come they advance and enhance their financial status and benefits, although sometimes they rarely meet the expectations of new employers? Why exactly does the media warm up to them and the players enjoy training with them? What is it that sets them apart from their colleagues? Some would say it's charisma, others would add they closely follow modern trends, and perhaps somehow manage to create more of a connection with the players. It may be to do with having better contacts or knowing more influential people. Elements of the truth may be found in all of these answers.

You'll find the answer to these questions in this chapter. Unlike the first four chapters, which are more focused on the theory of mentioned topics, this one consists of practical experience about issues, which are usually not part of the skills taught. And these side-issues often make a difference in being an average or successful coach.

Set Goals Are an Expression of a Common Pursuit

Its a kind of art form to build a successful team in sport. Not even the greatest coaches in the world succeed overnight, and for sure, I'm not exaggerating when describing the process of creating a team. I know, it's not a coach's game, but it is a player's game. Although it's the players who are physically playing, the coach is the one who holds a clear vision of the game and the team and transforms it into practice with the players. The coach must help players to fully understand what it means to be a team. He needs to encourage players to realize the team's common success is a multiplied result of their individual successes. When they're encouraged in this way, when players feel that they're better than the other team, this can only be recognized and rewarded. It takes time to form "the team." It's a painstaking process of creation and sacrifice. When you manage to make the players support one another, you've already completed most of the work, as the process can only continue to build and spread positively. A successful coach thinks highly of his players, recognizes and respects their individuality, including the personality of players and equally their private lives. Players should always be spoken to as equals on all issues. Players simply need to feel that they're important. When you speak to them, you need to point out their tasks and their specific roles as well as your expectations. The set goals of a team should be perceived by players as an expression of a common pursuit. The most fundamental aspect players need to understand is that the team always wins, not the individual. Individual success within a team is to be welcomed, but it's more important what the entire team is going to do. When you're accepted by the players, when they are convinced of your honesty and fairness, their anger, caused by a substitution on the pitch or not being picked for the starting 11, disappears. Pay attention to what players under a successful coach point out in their interviews or statements: "I'm just one link in the chain;" "I would never have succeeded if my play hadn't been supported by my team mates."

Analysis Kicks Off the Working Week

The working week of a coach usually begins with a meeting with colleagues before the first training session after the game. This is primarily about performing the analysis of the previous match. Only after that can a meeting with the players be held. Analysis of the game should never be too long nor too varied and has to have a dual character: psychological and technical-tactical. The psychological approach to the players mainly depends on the outcome of the last match. After defeat, the coach must strive to raise the morale of the team as a whole as well as that of the individuals. Following victory, the coach must "keep the team firmly on the ground," and not allow players to be affected by the euphoria. During the analysis, none of the players should be individually named, criticized, or publicly blamed for the defeat or negative play. These can be possibly presented to each individual player face-to-face in private. I once knew a coach who would never criticize players after a defeat, but instead only after a victory. Also, he never criticized the subs or younger players. He had a positive attitude toward them, encouraging their qualities. He told me he discovered such an approach proved to be successful. And when I think about it, it seems to me that his approach makes perfect sense. Additionally, I've always found analysis after a victory to be harder. Why? Because euphoria after a victory, heavily influenced by the fans and the environment created by the players, always results in poor play or defeat in the next match. As for technical and tactical analysis, based on statistical data prepared by his assistants, the coach is obliged to point out the flaws during the game, but also to point out the good side, publicly giving praise to individuals for following his instructions during the game.

After defeat, a coach always needs to be accountable in the eyes of the public. He should never look for an excuse for failure, either personal or on behalf of the players. The coach is always responsible for choosing the optimal playing system, the team selection, the organization, and training load. Such an approach is appreciated and respected among players. After the analysis of the match is complete, the coach and his expert team begin to prepare for the next match. Players have to become familiar with the plan and schedule for the current week, gradually getting to know their next opponent and the way they play. And so the first training session of the new working week begins together with the process of psychological and motivational preparation of the team for the upcoming match.

Are Coaches Always Right?

Most coaches want to be right all the time. At the place where I was born there is a saying: "If a man is right 55 percent of the time, he can be considered as a great man."

So, of course, the coaches also cannot be right all the time. But there are some small tips and tricks that can be used to achieve what they want. If as a coach you want to convince your players that certain training exercises can be done better, you should never say "I'll prove to you that this can be done better!" This is the same as telling them, "You'd better listen to me, because I'm smarter than you." Defiance and conflict among players and a toxic atmosphere in the dressing room is created by these words. Players should be taught without even noticing. You also have to be careful when you persuade the media about something you're not one hundred percent sure of. You'll never embarrass yourself if you honestly admit that you may be wrong. And if you're sure your interlocutor is wrong, don't give him a rough time. You won't achieve anything at all.

A few years ago, today's head coach of the Croatian National soccer team Zlatko Dalic was with his then club, Al-Tain FC, in a friendly match during a break in Turkey. In the 50th minute he replaced Ismail Ahmed with the young player Mohanad Salem in the belief that his quality would accelerate the flow of the ball. It didn't happen. They lost the match. Following the match, during an interview, one of the journalists blamed him for the defeat. Coach Zlatko Dalic didn't like it and tried to justify his move to the journalist. The next day during a regular scheduled press conference, the Croatian coach knew he'd be asked the same question by certain journalists. He decided to change his attitude. When the question about the substitution arose, he refrained from justifying himself and humbly replied, "To be honest, I can see now that I was wrong. I'm sorry I made this substitution." Miraculously nobody asked any more questions about the substitution, nor was it mentioned in the media ever again. So, we all can learn throughout our lives. Zlatko Dalic learned that if you want people to conform to your way of thinking, you must respect the opinion of others.

Coaches Make Mistakes, Don't They?

Mistakes are an inevitable part of life. If you make mistakes, it means you're active and alive. Mistakes should be accepted as part of life. Mistakes should be always turned to our advantage, and we shouldn't blame others for them. If you did something wrong, you should think about it deeply and analyze what went wrong. Why did this mistake happen to me? Did I act without thinking? Did I hesitate too long and lose sight of exactly what I was doing? Was I distracted and in turn did something stupid? The most important aspect of all this is to recognize and admit your mistakes and then to do everything it takes not to repeat them. As a coach, difficulties arise that are simply part of the job. A coach can either solve or suppress them. What does it mean to suppress them? This means that mistakes are distorted, denied, and shown in an opposite way from what they truly are, moved into an easier context. We like to philosophize and theorize about mistakes. All of us sometimes like to bluff others into believing in our success and strength when, in fact, the most difficult thing for us is to solve problems. The most primitive form of suppression is denial. Problems should never be transferred from difficult to easy opponents or from tricky away fixtures to comfortable home fixtures in the belief that better results will be achieved against a weaker opposition, or at home. Some coaches blame their players for failure. Pointing the finger at players is the worst move a coach can make. This is only a short-term solution. Problems mustn't be suppressed or left to someone else to solve them instead. We need to roll up our sleeves and get to work. Problems won't be miraculously solved by themselves. We're the only ones to solve them. And yes, mistakes can be a great teacher and fertile ground for personal development, as I was assured by my friend, amateur soccer coach Zeljko Orehovec. Although not a professional, he has a very conscientious and meticulous approach to coaching. Each time he came to a new club or before the start of the season, he would carefully outline specific goals. The process of achieving these goals was to split them into certain timeframes or stages, the so-called milestones. After the completion of each stage, such as the preparation cycle, at certain parts of the season he made a brief analysis, carefully comparing the results achieved to the targeted objectives. As he had a habit of re-reading his notes from time to time, he noticed that certain errors were constantly being repeated, so he began to correct them. He also noticed, based on his notes that the same players would always get yellow or red cards, and the same ones would, sure enough, always rebel and so on. To analyze everything, according to him, was not an easy task, but thanks to his additional education and discussion with older colleagues, he managed to keep his mistakes, including mistakes in his relationships with his players to a minimum. Today he's a successful and highly sought-after amateur coach, primarily due to the "significant" correction of his own mistakes.

A Persuasive Technique to Reach Physical Strength

The physical strength of players is one of the most important aspects of sports training. Going back to physical training from my playing days, I still fondly remember today how my coach used to ride a bicycle alongside us as we'd take on a 12-kilometer run from the stadium to the nearby river. One thing's for sure; thanks to such physical training, a player can become a good runner, but it's doubtful he could become a highly prepared soccer player. So it's understandable that I later spent quite a lot of time talking about the importance of a player's physical conditioning and that I've also learned something. My former club teammate, and today's coach of the one of the top Asian soccer club Persepolis FC, Branko Ivankovic, was also taught in this very same way. Yet he was determined to come up with a fitness regime specifically tailored for soccer players. Something totally different from our coach on two wheels. The physical fitness of players has to be specific in relation to soccer. Although Ivankovic's fitness regime is varied, appealing and mainly linked to the ball, I noticed that it nevertheless falls hard on the players. This is actually a normal reaction. Players always find it hard when the training load is increased. To alleviate such a reaction, for several years Branko Ivankovic has used a motivational technique using the power of persuasion prior to training. It consists of persuading the individual players and as a group that conditional preparation is necessary to achieve the ultimate success of the team, and to keep the continuity of playing well without injury. As the season unfolds he always tries not to overload players with conditional training, yet equally not to neglect it. During the season, he never overloads players to the limits of their physical endurance. For many years now, since working with professional clubs, a segment of physical conditioning of his team is led by a specialist, who plays an essential role in his professional team. Regardless of how much he appreciates his assistant's expertise, Branko Ivankovic still makes the call at his own discretion about the required training load of the players. His assistant, a specialist in physical training, has the green light to fully decide the best way to achieve this desired load.

Self-Control with Things Out of Your Influence

In my opinion, soccer really is the most beautiful sport in the world. It brings joy, pleasure, generosity, hope, and even faith. Despite these sets of values, a large number of coaches, due to their enormous, constant desire to win every single game, find it a challenge to relax and enjoy its charms. Soccer would not be soccer if everyone would constantly win. Unnecessary nervousness in these coaches usually floats to the surface while leading the team in a game. I like to observe coaches during a match. It's fascinating to see how every coach goes through the course of a game in his own different way. Some coaches are noisy and nervous. Others sit on the bench completely calm, and some are always on two feet, standing. I really do worship coaches who seem to stay calm and who can experience the play of their team stress-free. You must be wondering how come certain coaches manage to stay calm during a match full of twists and surprises? Well, this is because they intensively prepare before every match throughout the entire week, so there's no need to additionally influence the players during the match. In particular, no jumping and shouting in front of the bench.

If the coach creates a scene and constantly shouts out comments, he creates a negative impact on the younger players, and in turn they cannot fully concentrate on the game due to the fear of making a mistake, but they constantly listen to what the coach is shouting. On the other hand, coaches who are calm can be often judged by the public and the club management as having a far too laid back attitude toward the interests of the club. This is simply not true. Within the football world, there are many coaches who cannot maintain self-control on aspects they simply cannot influence—referees, the crowd, and the pitch. The simple logic indicates that this is an unnecessary exhaustion. The same applies to cases when coaches indulge in unnecessary expert analysis and discussion with those who lack expert knowledge. Therefore, my advice to coaches is whenever a soccer "know-it-all" wants to start a discussion about the tactics of the team, the game system, or even the changes made—you should immediately think of the wise words of the great writer Mark Twain who said "never argue with ignorant people, they will drag you down to their level and beat you with experience" (www.economist.com).

Don't worry about this. People who know how to play are not sitting on the bench; they're sitting in the stands! That's how it's always been and how it'll stay. That's the beauty of soccer. Soccer isn't played because of us, but for those who look forward to the goals.

Noticing Little Things Creates Tactical Dominance

Not everyone shares the same gift of perception. Some evaluate the gift of perception as insignificantly small. When I think about coaching virtues, the gift of perception ranks highly. Lucidity of mind, observational ability, and quick decision-making are not only skills needed for pilots and soldiers but also for coaches. After watching a 90-minute soccer match, a regular viewer would hardly remember all the disputable details, all the scoring opportunities, and all the attacks. Unlike those, the coaches fall into the category of people who have the power of detailed observations. A coach who has developed detailed perception skills penetrates into the depths of all the missed opportunities and the opponent's tactics. The sharp power to observe the rival's game has brought victory to certain coaches, and I certainly know many who use this virtue as a good basis to explain why the match was lost. Over the last decade, coaches have paid particular attention to analysis. Together with their expert team, they involve players in the analysis of the game, analyzing their rivals, their weaknesses and strengths. You wouldn't believe how important the power of perception can be when going through this in-depth process. Sometimes just noticing a minor detail can create a strategic victory. Don't fall into the trap of thinking our opponents fail to analyze us and our game. Today, everyone is aware of everything, so often little things, such as the power of perception, dominate. He who masters the trivia knows how to master greater things. Only those who notice even the smallest mistakes can be expected not to put up with the larger ones. Small or large, important or not, coaches usually realize only after the consequences. What entails serious consequences is never a minor issue, no matter how insignificant it seems to us at that particular moment.

Positive Atmosphere Vital for Success

The success of a certain club doesn't solely depend on those outstanding players and insightful coaches. It also depends on the specific atmosphere and communication culture at the club. If all these factors are combined and a family atmosphere is nurtured, the success of the club won't be far behind. Comparing previous clubs where I've played and worked, it's evident that in some, there was a lack of positive atmosphere. This was mostly due to the lack of communication culture of the people who led these clubs. Many can identify with the terms "club culture" and "climate," although they are two very different terms. The atmosphere shared in a sports club is a short-term situation depending on the club's leadership style and current results. A positive atmosphere draws large crowds to stadiums with a desire to have a good time, cheering for their favorites. For days, people would talk about the goals, scores, and the highlights of every match. The club atmosphere, whether positive or negative, is directly influenced by the way the club is managed. It's formed mainly by those who run the club—presidents, directors, and, of course, coaches.

Do you think the media plays a part in all this?

The media doesn't create the club atmosphere; it merely transfers it to the interested public. Unlike the short-term phenomenon of club atmosphere, club culture is a long-term process, created over the years. It forms the environment in which players, coaches, and others connected with the club work. A common part of club culture is the wall featuring pictures of club legends in the VIP Room, sharing the message of showing how much the club values its past and how much it means in terms of pride.

The working environment depends on communication, and many often neglect the fact that the club's communication is not only about discussion among the club's staff, but equally communication etiquette, the club's image, appearance, and respect for tradition. I did too, as an insignificant club employee, fully respect that. However, unfortunately many of our colleagues simply don't recognize that in order to bring crowds to the stadium and to significantly attract potential sponsors, not only are sports results crucial, but equally important is the tradition, a positive atmosphere, and the communication climate that flows in and around the club.

Should A Coach Believe Everything
His Assistants Say?

Modern training and team management requires teamwork. And the only organizer and coordinator of these activities is the head coach. As a head coach, you have your assistants, and it's common that your daily team of associates consists of two training assistants, a doctor, and a physiotherapist. Of course, this doesn't apply to the coaches of amateur clubs, but to the more professional teams if they can afford it. An expert team is usually made up of competent, professional people who elaborate strategic and tactical ideas, preparing players for the match. The coach's professional team in a professional club has a clearly defined goal. It's common to all and completely clear. Each member of the team knows his responsibilities and what he has to do. At the same time, the team shouldn't consist of individuals who are individually doing things in their own way. The success of a team is always above the ambitions of individual team members. Do these things function like this in reality also? The establishment and operation of a professional sport team is a very demanding job together with hard work. This is because different ambitions appear in different teams. For example, it happens often that a kit man clearly notices when assistants, driven by personal ambition, obstruct the work of the coach. They just imagine they're better than him. The professional team must be a well-chosen squad with high-quality loyal assistants. The worst examples for me are when assistants give support to any proposal from the head coach, and then after just one defeat, the entire blame is on him. Driven by a similar issue, a friend of mine, famous Croatian soccer coach Branko Ivankovic, once sacked his assistant with an interesting explanation: "He was an assistant who always agreed with my opinion and suggestions. We would never disagree on anything. I don't want to keep paying him just to hear my own opinion." In a good team there are no secrets. Everyone knows what's going on, whether it's good or bad. All team members are ready and competent to express their views and differences of opinions, without fear of upsetting the team leader—the head coach. In an effort to avoid possible unnecessary conflict, it's common practice for the head coach to agree with all team members on the performance standards during the formation of his expert team. After this, team members know what the head coach and, equally, the club, expects from them. This increases the performance of the team and reduces the likelihood of conflict. In successful professional teams, there are really no secrets. Everyone knows what's happening and the potential consequences.

There's complete openness and honesty from each team member. The unwritten rule of work of such teams is "together we stand and together we fall!"

Say, Point, and Include the Players

Each training session, match, competition, or meeting with the players requires the coach's careful preparation. The way a coach conveys information regarding the opponents, the competition, or the game are key. And what would you say how much players actually remember from all of this? You'd be surprised!

According to the National Highway Institute, adults retain approximately 10 percent of what they see, 30–40 percent of what they see and hear, and 90 percent of what they see, hear, and do (https://thepresentationdesigner.co.uk).

What Can We Conclude From This?

The spoken word of a coach has the least impact on the players. The spoken word along with visual instructions has a moderate effect. Interestingly, the coach's spoken words together with visual instructions and actively engaging the players in discussion, by far, achieves the maximum effect. Therefore I strongly advise coaches to enrich their preparation for competition or training with images, graphics, or even video footage. If the players are actively included in the whole story, the success of the team is on its way! This theoretical knowledge has been put into practice for many years by leading coaches around the world. And coach's assistants certainly won't be too enthusiastic about hearing this. In fact, it's them who'll have to carry and take care of all the technical equipment needed and these are sometimes difficult to transfer from the bus to the plane, and from one match to another match.

The Power of Positive Thinking

"Whether you think you can, or you think you can't, you're right" (Henry Ford; www.forbes.com). This beautiful thought of Henry Ford, the founder of the Ford Motor Company, confirms that by using a positive approach, anything can be achieved. The same goes for winning a match. If we think we can do something, with a positive outlook our odds increase. A positive attitude opens a boundless source of motivation directed toward success and victory. We should always try to think positive! Most people don't take this recommendation seriously. I'm not sure whether they understand what it really means or they just see it as useless and ineffective. Aren't all of us who play or used to play some sports in the team convinced that even if our opponent scored the game isn't over, but more so at the moment when we think we might lose? Positive thinking is a mental attitude that filters into our thoughts, words, and images that contribute to growth, development, and success. Positive thinking presupposes happiness, joy, health, and the ability to overcome any situation. Everything our mind searches for, it finds. Positive as well as negative thinking is contagious. All of us, in one way or another, influence the people we meet, in the same way coaches influence their players. This happens instinctively and unconsciously through our thoughts, feelings, and body language. People want to be surrounded by positive people and avoid negativity! If you're positive, players will be willing to help in achieving the set goals. Negative thoughts, words, and attitudes lead to dissatisfaction, failure, and ultimately, disappointment. In order to become successful and popular in coaching work, one has to think positive, as positive thinking is conveyed to the players. The power of thinking is a powerful force that shapes our lives. This usually happens subconsciously but the process can be implemented consciously. Therefore, coaches have to believe in every player and expect a positive outcome to every match. With such an attitude you can't lose, you only gain. If negative thoughts enter your mind, you should try to get rid of them as soon as possible and replace them with positive concepts. If you feel somewhat resistant to adopting a more positive outlook, you shouldn't give up and continue to look for useful, good, and happy thoughts inside your mind. Our positivity must be constantly obvious, especially when communicating with players. In relation to player–coach communication, positivity is most commonly expressed through providing feedback to the players. Player feedback shouldn't include criticism, but eventually focus on expressing dissatisfaction with the players' behavior. Feedback should be a form of analysis of activities or the behavior of a certain player in order to help him improve. When communicating to the player, it's important to always stay focused on what can be changed, rather than stick to things that might be taken as an attack on the individual's personality.

Self-Confidence Can Be Crucial in Swaying the Odds

The other day I read the title on my mobile phone: "Penalties have not dampened Rashard Robinson's self-confidence" (www.nbcsports.com). But do you actually know what it means to be self-confident? Psychologists describe self-confidence as a dimension of self-awareness that is reflected in one's conviction of having those traits that make him/her competent to always have full control over the results of their activities, to adjust them to what he/she appreciates and considers desirable (Havelka 1992). The theory of self-esteem is defined as confidence in yourself and your possibilities. A high level of confidence is manifested through a high degree of confidence in one's own judgment, or a high opinion of one's self-worth. This means that a coach who is full of confidence is one who believes completely in his own professional knowledge, skills, and abilities. We can all agree with that, can't we? Such a coach always, both directly and indirectly, transfers his confidence to the team, motivating the players to exploit their potential to the fullest. A confident coach transfers a positive attitude and spreads optimism among players. Coaches who are full of confidence are not averse to risk-taking and taking responsibility in the most critical moments of the game. They accept each difficult situation as a challenge. Self-confidence is certainly one of the significant factors distinguishing successful from less successful coaches. Most coaches have excellent technical knowledge, but often fail to cross the border to genuine excellence. Why? One of the key reasons is that they're not sure of their abilities and capabilities, not using them at critical moments when it's most needed for the team. They never take risks, always opting for a safer option. You're probably wondering where exactly the problem lies? In the head; it's all in the head. Coaches with low confidence must overcome their psychological barriers and start believing in themselves, in their knowledge, skills, and abilities. It might mean abandoning the usual security, but for sure, if we don't change ourselves, we won't progress. So I'll repeat once again that coaches who have a far better chance on the road to success speak steadily, behave properly, look appropriate, and are always in a good mood. Simply, in a nutshell, those who've mastered the skill of verbal and non-verbal communication radiate with confidence, before they've even said their first word.

Always "Fair Play"

All of us who are involved with sport, either as coaches, players, staff, fans, or sponsors, should have a highly developed awareness of ethics and ethical behavior. Ethics in sport dictates the relationship we have with ourselves and with others in a way that everybody is satisfied. "'Fair play" is one of the most important categories of ethics in sport. The founder of the modern Olympic Movement, Pierre de Coubertin, firmly believed "fair play" had a special place in sport and ethics. Did you know that the Declaration of Human Rights of the United Nations states: "All human beings are born free and equal in dignity and rights" (www.un.org/). This is a big deal. Coaches should teach this to players from an early age, so, regardless of being in competition or in conflict, they'd always remember this statement. "Fair play" and the fight to stamp out racism in sport should be seen as the greatest moral value of sport, as a guarantee of fair competition, acceptance of the rules, and respect for the sport. To respect "fair play" means to respect and abide by its rules. In a club where "fair play" is fostered, you'll always find honesty, safety, and a passion for justice. To behave fairly with your opponent means to be tolerant and calm.

The opposite of "fair play" represents fraud and cheating, inconsistency, violence, hatred, discrimination, and disrespecting the rules. Coaches whose only philosophy is to be top of their league often dare to question fairness and violate the rules of the game. "Fair play" is not just a sports term, it's also a synonym for reasonable behavior in everyday life. Unfortunately, and you probably know it, the reality is not always in the spirit of "fair play." Within many clubs, coaches are met with hatred, jealousy, gossip, and disrespect. Evidence for this can be easily found. There are coaches who'll try to win at all costs, even to sacrifice their defensive player, instructing him to injure the opposing attackers, regardless of the consequences. There are also examples around the world where in major competitions, famous players, contrary to the rules, score a point or goal using, for example, their hand in soccer, and then deny it ever happened. The ideals of "fair play" should constantly shine in the work of a coach. A successful coach appreciates sport, the game, and the athletes regardless of skin color and religion, follows the rules, and strictly plays fairly. He knows that it's the only right way to practice sport and the only satisfaction guaranteed after competition and training. So, the coaches should respect "fair play," always strive to do their best at every training session and competitive game, accept and support the sports rules and the message it represents. A coach, player, or team whose commitment, desire to win with creativity and ability are strong, should always be congratulated at the end of the match, regardless of the outcome.

Each Crisis Means an Opportunity

There is a story about this topic I'd like to tell. The famous Croatian coach Drazen Besek had just taken over the reins of Chinese club Shanghai Shenhua. He was in a taxi on his way from his hotel to the stadium. Along the route he spotted a giant billboard with two big Chinese letters. He was intrigued so he asked the taxi driver what they meant. The taxi driver explained that together they mean "a crisis," but if read individually, the first means "danger" and the second "opportunity." Within European culture, in which the two of us grew up, a crisis in a term is traditionally seen as a problem or an obstacle. Undoubtedly, Chinese traditional culture is far more creative compared to Europe! For the Chinese, a crisis means just as much danger as a good opportunity. Due to the nature of their work, coaches work with crisis situations on a daily basis and therefore need to be familiar with crisis communication. Two defeats in a row and the absence of the crowd favorite from the starting 11 are issues that can easily lead the coach to a crisis situation. Statistics show that coaches who failed to communicate well during a crisis situation were often let go in just a few days, tarnishing their reputation on the way. Of course, there are positive examples when coaches strategically manage the crisis thanks to excellent communication.

Having learned this Chinese story about my friend, it is clear that every single crisis for a coach always means not only danger but a new opportunity. The crisis is, for example, an opportunity for a coach to obtain media coverage, which is otherwise hard to reach. And coaches should always be prepared for a crisis situation and the media interest that it attracts. As public figures, coaches actively participate in the public life of the community. So it's normal to be accountable for their work and, likewise, the media interest they attract in a crisis situation is completely understandable. Media experts point out that in a crisis, the first 24 hours are crucial. During this period, the pressure from the media toward the coach is at its peak, as the public curiosity begins to grow. The way a coach communicates in the first 24 hours reveals how capable and trained he is to deal with the challenge. A crisis in sport after few matches lost in a row is a normal thing that eventually every coach needs to deal with. How can a coach handle the situation following a string of poor results? Coaches shouldn't deny their responsibility. Taking responsibility doesn't mean recognition of guilt, which, unfortunately, many coaches fail to grasp. Coaches must understand the media's hunger for information. They don't need to hide away from the media, turning off their mobile phones. Based on my own experience, I would strongly suggest avoiding press conferences in the first couple of days after the outbreak of a crisis. Why? Communication via press conferences puts every coach in front of a "firing squad" with the attack of all sorts of questions, some quite uncomfortable and awkward, so it's far better to avoid them. During a crisis period, the smartest advice is to give affirmative statements, without further excuses or blame, or to use a positive notion to overshadow fresh negative news. I would recommend, if your club gives the "green light," completing your expert team with a communications specialist. He'll certainly know what to do and greatly advise you on how to communicate during a crisis. Don't forget that all coaches are under quite a lot of pressure and anxiety levels are high during a crisis situation, and their thoughts are more or less subjective.

The Managerial Merry-Go-Round

In most soccer nations, including here in Europe, after a series of consecutive defeats, it's common practice to see a change of head coach. I wonder why has this preferred solution by club management become the norm. Usually because after the coach comes in, the result-oriented effect of the team immediately increases. But, in most cases, this growth trend is short-lived. During the first weeks following the change of the coach, players closely watch the new one. They're obedient, trying to create an impact, with maximum engagement. On the other hand, the new coach wants to be seen in the most positive light possible. He wants to show his knowledge and competence to the players, and to gain their trust. He searches for the ideal team, asking players to fight for their position. Players, who once had certain credibility with the former coach, become just equal contenders for the first 11 (soccer) with the new one. Once the first team squad has crystallized, there's a time of stabilization. Those who don't feature in the first "11" or "18" immediately harbor negative views about the coach. If the team doesn't recognize the new coach's "strength" or him as a person who can help achieve their goals, he won't do well. If however, a new coach manages to impose his expertise, integrity, and approach on the players, his position becomes stable and he can expect a competitive breakthrough. Why? Players surrender themselves unconditionally to the coach they've accepted. They warm up to his decisions and his method of managing the team, which leads to long-term success. Players' belief in the coach's competence can greatly influence the overall strength of the team. Nevertheless, if the results turn, and things don't go the way of the club, a change is on the cards. So the coach's bags should always be ready, right?

What Do People Think of You?

Have you ever been haunted by the thought, "What people think of me?" "What would they say if I picked Roy instead of Paul?" If you aim to become a top coach, you'll never bother with what people say about your work. You should worry about what your conscience says. To follow your conscience means you're a coach with a strong character. The largest obstacle in building a strong character is the fact that it can't be built overnight. This is always a slow process. Maturing ourselves takes hard work of a lifetime. Today's major obstacle in building a strong character is the continued fast pace of life and running after achievements of material value. Within a blink of an eye, a huge number of coaches can tell you the names the first 11 of their opposing teams, but in terms of their own character, they'll struggle to say a few words as they've probably failed to recognize who they actually are. Character cannot be built without knowing ourselves, without learning and constant development. This is normal as success can't be reached without victims and sacrifices. The best example of this is the coaching profession itself. Getting up early in the morning to get ready for training, having lunch, and then back to the training pitch once again. During the evening more match analysis, training preparation for the next day, and so on. This repeats day after day. It's the same with our character.

To build your own character, you need to invest a huge amount of persistence and premeditated work. Don't ever complain or justify why you're this or that, why you're passionate, temperamental, or have a short fuse. Your seemingly untamed passion and fiery temperament can be nurtured with practice. Everything is simply a matter of desire, exercise, and training. Those that give up easily usually say "I'm this way by nature. That's how I was born." This certainly isn't true. To back this up, I always remember the late president of the club where I started my career. After drinking just a few glasses of alcohol, he'd unfortunately turn into an unpleasant and confrontational beast. As a very clever man, he immediately recognized his drinking issues and worked hard to address them. He then gave up alcohol. Even today, I admire the positive strength of his character. Everything can be achieved if there's a real desire and it's never too late for a man to become the man he wants to be!

The Person I Am

Regardless of the level of competency or expertise of a coach, the players and sports public see him first as a person. If they don't like him as a person, they won't like him as a coach, despite his knowledge and skills.

Besides giving a positive answer to the question, "What kind of an expert am I?," a coach is also expected to answer the question, "What kind of person am I?" Do you know how much time you've devoted to your personal development? Believe me when I say that only development in both segments results in achieving a successful coaching career! As coaches, you all tend to invest additional time and money to enhance your knowledge about technique, tactics, and physical training, yet only a few of you are willing to go ahead and invest in personal development. Equally, without having both sets of expertise, you can't become a strong and successful coach. Talking about a coach, how many times have I heard players say:

> He's a great coach! He knows everything. But God forbid if he ever leads the training session. He doesn't know how to communicate. He's a really tough person and unable to cooperate. He's always right, shouting, and never listens to anyone!

The professional quality of these coaches will never come to light as they've never learned fundamental human communication skills. A coach will never become successful based only on his knowledge of technique, tactics, and physical preparation. If you want to become a successful coach, along with your expertise, you have to master and fine-tune your communication skills. You have to open the doors of your spirituality. The adoption of communication skills and the impact on people is extremely important for coaches, as well as the kind of impression it leaves. The same applies to players. Players, who develop in just a professional capacity, fail to achieve the best results. Top players become those who, along with having the talent and sports skills, understand and appreciate human relationships in the team.

The Crucial Role of a Coach in Conflict Situations

Coaches don't like conflict. They'll do everything they can to avoid tension in the changing rooms. Naturally conflict with players or colleagues isn't good at all and should be avoided at all costs. No matter how bad things become, sometimes the consequences for the team can be useful. There's never complete harmony in the team. Soccer is a game where only

11 actually play. The apparent team harmony only lasts for as long as the team is winning. With the first defeat the first signs of tension come along. The role of a coach in a conflict situation is therefore crucial. He has to use his authority and competence to maintain the unified spirit of his team. What does that actually mean? This means a coach must be decisive and be open to cooperation and compromise. If through conflict a coach turns out to be in the wrong, he has to be reasonable and willing to accept his mistake, and ready to listen and consider a better proposal. It's obvious that different situations require different procedures from coaches. It might happen that there is a situation where players' suggestions to resolving a problem are better than those of the coach.

A well-sought quality of a coach is the willingness to accept things, even when he may not be pleased with it. I know it's a terrible kick to the ego, especially when it comes from a player. When you listen to something that you don't like, don't immediately defend or deny it and try to stay away from sarcasm. In conflict situations, always trying to emphasize the importance of the contribution of the entire team in order to achieve the club's goals is always more important than the achievement of the individual targets of disgruntled players or coaches.

Don't Justify Defeat

"We wouldn't have lost if our top player had played." Looking for excuses after a defeat is a desperate move! There are many coaches who want to justify their failure with the recent challenges they've faced. Do you think a problem, such as top player not playing, is a valid excuse for the team's defeat? Have you ever thought that maybe you as a coach are the one most accountable for the defeat? Why not find an appropriate replacement? You didn't find it, but you immediately found a good excuse in his absence. It seems to me that failure in this case was set in advance, even before the game started. I'll tell you an interesting story I read on the subject. Once you hear it, you'll never look for an excuse after defeat again. When Dwight Eisenhower, the supreme commander of the Allied forces in World War II, left his military service, he became the rector of the University of Columbia in New York. One day a student approached him, asking to change the exam time, because he wasn't feeling well. He asked to postpone the scheduled time because he simply wanted more time to prepare better. Eisenhower asked: "Have you been unwell perhaps?" The student then replied: "I wasn't sick, but I've been feeling bad." "Dear friend," he answered as he turned toward the other students, "Most of the great and significant actions in the world were done by people who had been in a bad mood or even sick. Due to being unwell some were even more hard-working, as they felt their time was numbered to achieve their plans. So I openly say: if me and my soldiers had done whatever we liked, things that only made us happy, we would never have won the Second World War. However, since we were all completely committed to the hard work we had to do, and persevered in severe difficulties, we ultimately won freedom for the whole world" (Srica 2003). I'm convinced Eisenhower's message is a good example of how every difficulty can and must be transformed into a surge of motivation. It's not easy, but that is precisely the secret of success. Successful people don't allow themselves to be broken by all sorts of problems. They use them as motivation toward the goals they set. It doesn't matter whether you've let in a goal, whether you're down to ten men, or even if your best players are injured. It's important you stay in the game. You need to have the drive to want to score and to win. In sport, we face constant challenges and ultimately it's up to you and your athletes to make the decision to surrender and give up, or win. In sport it's specifically these difficulties faced by coaches that should become the highest possible motivation. So, the next time you're thinking of justifying yourself, bite your tongue and simply continue to do what you are doing. You'll see that the "expected" defeat will turn into victory.

The Greatness of a Coach Shines Through in Tough Times

Human greatness is best seen in difficult situations. The coaching profession is a perfect reflection of this. In times of challenges, conflicts, and hardships our true nature is best expressed. It's not easy to be great both in victory and defeat. What's the best way to react following defeat? What should you do when the media, fans, or club's board pile on the pressure and swoop down on you like hornets? Hardly any coach during tough times can think about stress. You usually start focusing on stress when you begin to feel the first signs of health problems. So, what exactly are the symptoms of stress? You usually notice certain physical symptoms such as feeling discomfort, fast breathing, a pounding heart, and higher levels of anxiety. The typical stress situation for a coach is a press conference after a defeat. You know what you are in for in front of the press. It's like heading toward a firing squad of journalists who were thirsty for your blood. And usually there is not enough time to put together any sort of analysis of the match, and to reflect in peace about the specific reasons for the defeat. Just like many things in life, solutions can be solved by exercise and training. A few breathing techniques might help to stay very calm and self-composed. Try to reduce the scope and content of the information that you would otherwise generously share with the journalists. Using this approach, and without giving names and pointing the finger, the window of opportunity for journalists to throw in additional questions and create bombastic headlines is reduced. Avoid at any price off-the-wall statements, which usually cause offence to someone. Such a statement would spark a whole host of reactions, so instantly you'd become the topic of conversation for the entire week. Not to mention the next training session addressing the tense players who were casually mentioned in this statement.

Using this approach you'll see that's all a matter of practice and working on yourself. Success, happiness, and inner peace can't be achieved by itself. Everything comes from the right, positive thinking.

No Success Without Parental Cooperation and Support

Regularly meeting parents and explaining what would be the best thing for their budding little players is very important. I think a child shouldn't be introduced to the training process before the age of seven. The most important thing at preschool age is to develop affection toward the sport and training through the game. This process takes more than a single coach. It takes a number of coaches who work with children at the earliest age. It's really important a coach knows the child's parents, because there's no success without parental cooperation and support. All parents want the best for their child and at no time must they feel their child isn't in good hands. The parents should be spoken to often, as they should be aware that it's not only important for their child to become a good football player, but equally a good person. Often, this isn't easy as there are parents who simply don't understand the sport, who already see their child playing soccer for, let's say New York Red Bulls. The idea behind the concept of each serious sport school, along with the training and development, should be the mandatory completion of secondary education. During this time, young athletes, together with their school obligations, should be involved in training or a competitive program four to five times a week. Often coaches and parents are thrilled with their child's outstanding sports skills, declaring him a great potential talent and future star. They quickly forget the perfect sport skills aren't the only talent a child must have to become a top-flight athlete. Sports talent also consists of perseverance, character, speed, and strength. I also remember an opposite case when a 14-year-old's parents wanted their son to join one of our under-age soccer teams. He was tall, extremely fast, and totally besotted with soccer. Much to his and his parents' regret, the difference in controlling the ball between him and the older players was dramatic. This clearly shows us that any attempt to involve a child in the serious soccer world after the age of 10 is simply unrealistic. Preferably, as soon as possible, young players should be involved in working alongside senior players as this is the fastest way for them to mature. It's strongly suggested that you often introduce the occasional talented junior to your training sessions and friendly matches. This is a very good way for young players to adapt as soon as possible to senior soccer and its demands.

Knowledge Is Vital for Success

It's often said that a coach is a man who says on Friday he knows what will happen on Saturday, while on Sunday he's explaining why it didn't happen. The coaching profession is no longer exclusively linked with the pitch, the individual, or even the team. Today, alongside the work on the technical and tactical elements, a coach has to communicate with the media, sponsors, and fans. He also needs to show to the players his own example on how to behave, how to appear, and how to represent yourself to the public. Knowledge of communication and marketing skills can help every coach. Don't forget that the mere fact that someone is a good coach is no longer a guarantee of success. Therefore, the constant personal development is a must! Knowledge is vital for success in any business, especially in a profession that involves working with people. Fortunately, we're in a time where more and more high-quality, educated coaches with a positive image are in high demand. Although they're not "cheap", they don't have a problem finding coaching positions. So you too can become one of them! By investing in knowledge, you're investing indirectly in your image. Although there's no major difference in creating the image of players and coaches, there are some specifics in creating the image of a coach. In order to become successful in any field, you have to be distinguished and set yourself apart from the others. Good communication of the coach opens the door to creating a positive image. Your decision on insisting everyone wears the same clothes is to be commended as this is also a form of communication. The uniform worn by the players creates a sense of a club member's security and a feeling of belonging to a group.

Do Coaches Earn Too Much?

We've now come to a touchy subject. Do coaches earn too much? Hmmm... The fact is coaches who work with children earn far too little. I'll try to express my opinion by sharing a story. When you've heard it, you'll understand my take on whether coaches earn too much.

One day, a rich merchant decided to commission an interesting painting from a painter. This specific painting was supposed to represent a rooster in the most perfect way possible. A few years went by since his order, with no sight nor word of the painter. As his anxiety and uncertainty grew, he went to discover what exactly had happened to the painter. He eventually found the painter, but there was no painting. The painter invited the merchant to sit down and started to work on his request. In 15 minutes the painting of the rooster was complete. It was beautiful, a real masterpiece. The merchant was sincerely struck by its beauty. When it was time to pay for the painting, the merchant was stunned at the huge sum the artist dared to ask for a job completed in such a short time. He was so angry and refused to pay. The painter then took the merchant to his room and showed him a pile of paper the height of a man. On each piece of paper was a painting of a rooster. "I've been painting these for three years to practice. Thanks to this, I've gained the skills to paint this divine, perfect painting in such a short time. And so I have to get paid for my work during the long preparation time," explained the painter. The merchant was convinced the painter was right and paid him for the painting (Srica 2003).

It's the same thing in the coaching career. It takes years and years of training and perseverance in order to eventually gain a well-deserved reward, which means charging for your long-term hard work.

Use Every Free Moment to Relax

When you talk about success to successful coaches, they usually say that success is based on hard work and complete dedication to the job. My years of experience give me the right to say the time needs to be devoted equally to yourself and to your family. The older and more experienced I get, the more I stick to it. Unlike before, I don't spend my whole day working. I began to devote more of my time to myself and my family. I've noticed that since making the change, my body and mind are constantly in shape. My philosophy in life is not to outdo others, but my previous achievements. And in order to be able to work on myself, I take advantage of every free moment to relax. Only now do I understand why my late father George kept on saying: "Rest more and don't be constantly at work. When you relax your worries will disappear on their own, whether you want them to or not." The most common moments of relaxation are those spent with family and friends. It's interesting to note that the best strategies and ideas from Croatian soccer coach Branko Ivankovic actually emerged during his time drinking tea with friends and his brothers, who are his most objective critics. So, as my father advised me, I do the same to you, urging you not to miss the opportunity to dedicate at least one hour per day to yourself. There are many ways to do this. It entirely depends on your mood and circumstances. Perhaps just spending time with family members or a visit to places you're interested in like an art gallery or museum. Maybe buy a ticket for a concert. Reading books or watching movies might be your thing. Something simple like our football chat over tea may be just what you need. Often this can be just talking with those close to you. These are various ways to recharge your batteries. An hour every day devoted purely to yourself will help clear your mind. Dedication to yourself will allow you to get rid of negative thoughts and become creative, calm, and collected.

The Public Fails to Understand Why Coaches Are Attacked

It is a common situation that after a lost match a coach exchanges harsh word with some of the club officials or even a club's president. This shouldn't be taken too personally. When you take things too personally, you're not able to look at the situation objectively. As soon as you get into conflict with someone and feel the surge of violent reactions, you have to learn to develop a shield in order to reject the negative attitude and harsh words directed at you. The secret to avoid unnecessary controversy and negative reaction is to be aware that in most cases people don't understand why they're being attacked, so you have to forgive them for that, and not react negatively. Or maybe you're convinced that the club's president understands the tactics? Coping with personal attacks was a lesson I've learned from the coach of the soccer club I used to work at. The club had a weak team at that time, but the president believed we simply didn't have such a strong team for a long time. After just one defeat he spoke about the coach in front of the press, saying that he didn't know how to manage the players, although he never actually played soccer, nor did he under-stand the game. Rather than let it go, the coach reacted violently. Coinci-dentally, the debate was observed by the club's psychologist. Once he was alone with the coach, instead of reacting and defending his argument, the psychologist advised him that in a case like this, he never needs to prove to another he's wrong and especially not the president of the club. Initially this dampens the mood of everyone present and also he wouldn't gain the upper hand and be regarded as smarter. Why not leave a man convinced that he's right and why embarrass him in front of other people? Situations like these should be avoided at any cost.

Coaches Need to Mature

A coach on a mission to succeed needs to understand the nature of team leadership. The ability to lead a team is determined by the greatness of the coach. Leading a professional sports team is a complex process that involves mastering an array of skills, from general knowledge, professional expertise, and pedagogy to communication. All these skills are barely acquired in a short period of time. Certainly not overnight, but with time and patience, all the necessary knowledge and skills can be gained by every coach. Every one of these skills can be learned and improved upon. Do freshly picked grapes turn into wine in just one day? Time is needed for grapes to mature. It's the same with sports coaches. Figuratively speaking, coaches also need to mature. Like many well-known and recognized coaching names, before you flourish you have to work in the shade. Doors open to anyone who's willing to take it. Like diamonds that are created under huge pressure, so coaches are created through many ordeals. Young coaches are often impatient and want to make their way into a great club overnight. Some often get lost and simply disappear from the coaching scene although many are highly talented. Why? The lack of experience, wisdom, and humility. The three virtues that can only be developed over time. These are very important elements to gain success in coaching, along with other necessary qualities and maturity.

Is Polite Behavior a Sign of Weakness?

Again an anecdote from my own experience. Not even two months had passed since the day my friend took over the Croatian soccer club, NK Rijeka. During a training session, the physio approached him with the message that the president of the club was waiting for him in his office. The tone of his voice and facial expression signaled something wasn't quite right. He was prepared for the worst. Tea was brought into the room and, without any small talk, they got straight to the nitty-gritty. "Coach, they tell me you're too polite in leading the team. You have to know that the players are bastards. You need to be firm and dynamic with them." Despite being alone, my friend was taken aback by his remark.

He reacted like lightning with a counterquestion, "Normally, you expect me to knock on the door before entering your office, and as I come in, it's normal to say 'Hello, how are you?' What would you think of me if I'd entered your office without even knocking, without a greeting, saying 'Hi, how can I help? Is civilized behavior to my players a sign of my weakness, a sign that I'm soft?" After his energetic and impulsive reaction, the club president was left speechless and then apologized to him. This story is a classic example of how a civilized and democratic leadership style has nothing to do with strength and discipline. We all know that leadership styles may vary. In theory, there are two styles widely accepted: autocratic and democratic. They are often considered as mutually exclusive. You belong to one or the other. But is it really like this? Can they both be integrated? I strongly believe they can! This is precisely what many coaches do. When working with your players you should always be a gentleman, but in terms of the way you lead the team, a balance is needed. If necessary, you need to be firm, soft, flexible, and adaptable and use the style that seems the most appropriate at the time. Your team leadership style depends very much upon the particular situation, the culture of the environment in which you perform, and the individual personalities of certain players. Asians, unlike Europeans, perceive criticism in a very emotional and devastating way. The criticism shared has to be tactful as it's very sensitive to criticize players in front of other members of the team. All issues with Asian players should be resolved in private, with lots of individual face-to-face discussion. Most coaches, who start work in Asia aren't aware of the subtleties and so often scandal is caused by their inappropriate statements. This is particularly true in China, Korea, and Japan, the Asian countries where the pressure to succeed is immense.

Reacting to Public Criticism

How many times have you found yourself in a situation feeling hurt due to criticism? I'm sure you've often thought for days about the harsh words or the sharp pen of a journalist. The eternal question that follows coaches is how to handle criticism. The answer depends on whether the criticism is justified and who is it from, although there are some coaches among you who are convinced no criticism whatsoever is justified.

If the criticism is justified, and expressed by people who know your work, you have to seriously take it into consideration. Opinions of the people who don't know you don't need to be regarded as so relevant, as they criticize the person they imagine you to be. They've created an opinion about you through media writings or your public appearances, either positive or negative, so you must understand this is something you simply cannot influence. I think every coach as a public figure should accept well in advance that his life or the work he does is going to provoke varied reactions in the public eye, which often end up with unfounded and inaccurate opinions. These are undeniable facts you have to be aware of. If you struggle to accept them, you'll be forced to constantly fight a losing battle. So, avoid correcting people in order to change their false beliefs, because it simply doesn't make sense. It's better to keep your head and save your time and energy for the people you can understand and enjoy communicating with. Sometimes it's even better to let people wallow in their ignorance, when their attitude has nothing in common with the truth than spend time and effort on unnecessary additional explanations. Everyone is entitled to a false belief, but equally you have the right to ignore such false beliefs. The public therefore has a right, not to have the right, but that doesn't mean they need to explain every wrong opinion or attitude. In my country, Croatia, there's a beautiful saying perfect for this: "If on your way, you look back at every barking dog, you'll never reach your goal." So, shortly, I suggest you don't bother with the critical opinions of people you don't know or the only thing left for you is to continue banging your head against the wall, wondering how your beautiful coaching job has turned into a nightmare.

When You Stop Pedaling, You Fall

The basis for successful performance in any job is a narrow specialization, which is only possible if you've got the specific expertise. Expert knowledge can't be gained over a short period, by attending a course or by obtaining a certain coaching qualification. The process of development of coaching expertise is ongoing; it can last a lifetime. Coaches who don't supplement their basic knowledge on a daily basis usually fade away, leaving the stadium with their heads down and disappear into the grayness of mediocrity. The education of sports coaches can be compared to cycling—the moment you stop pedaling, you fall. The moment you stop educating and investing in yourself, you disappear from the coaching scene. If you're not constantly mastering new skills and knowledge, you'll be overtaken by your younger colleagues, who'll be eager to jump into your place. The worst is when your work becomes routine, and your knowledge deteriorates. So keep renewing your knowledge continually. Study the literature, follow new trends, and analyze the work of your successful colleagues. You could occasionally take part in a seminar to upgrade both your personal and technical skills. Don't just follow sport. You should also follow other aspects of society and expand your horizons. You'll always find certain benefits in each area that can be applied to your coaching job. You wouldn't believe how much I've absorbed from motivational videos on YouTube from different sports. If you're only at the beginning, don't forget there are a lot of unfulfilled goals in front of you.

Achieving Prosperity Helps the Players

How many times have you been in a situation to help a fallen player but didn't do it? You thought the trouble would pass and time would heal the wounds. Today, you surely regret you missed the opportunity to help him, or at least hug him. For me, as I went through various temptations through my life, the most important thing I learned is that by helping others, I help myself the most. Players don't adore certain person, whether it is a coach or a club employee, for no reason. This is because if you are ready to help no matter what, if your attitude is smiling and joking it all comes back to you. As you help them, in turn they help you. Helping is infectious. It's the experience and talent of every person in every situation. I always wonder why coaches and players don't help each other more. Each one of them is always on the go, rushing somewhere, forgetting to stop, talk, and wait patiently. What a strange time we're living in! We've learned how to get rich, but we haven't learnt how to live. Our soul has been taken away by computers! We've ceased to communicate face-to-face. We want to gain respect and become successful overnight. Our communication has been reduced to e-mail, Facebook, or Twitter. It seems I can't keep up with the times! I keep wondering where on earth have human values disappeared to. If you want to build positive and friendly relationships with people, it's important to understand the purpose of support. Helping is not a waste of time! The moment you devote your time to a player, it's by no means a waste of time, but rather a great asset to you and the player. If you give a player the support, which may even be symbolic, a quick smile, a pat on the shoulder, or a hug, you're helping him to enhance an aspect of his life. When helping a player you're sending a message, expressing a positive attitude, understanding and caring about your player. Your message won't be left unnoticed. It also affects the other players, who'll copy you and start behaving in a similar way. The start of a positive atmosphere in the dressing room can be easily sparked with just one small gesture. Do you know how essential positive vibes in the dressing room are important for the coach as well? Priceless!

Players are often lost within the fog of the outside world, which knows no warm words, where helping words are unknown. Life that players face outside the stadium is, on the one hand, focused on the fight for a harsh existence and on the other making and spending money. As a coach you're able to spread kindness with a positive attitude and help others, but you also can spoil the mood of everyone around you with your miserable sourness. Well, the point is we shape our own attitude and we're able to manage it. Within the choice, you should choose a positive attitude. Help others and yourself and you'll be constantly happy.

Players Follow a Coach Out of Respect or Fear

In order to be followed obediently, admired, and respected by your players, you have to impose yourself as an authority. When appointed as a coach you became the formal authority, an authority by function. This authority is only temporarily accepted by the players. Over time, if you're not accepted by the players, your formal authority, given your function, will be ignored in a short space of time. Authority, unlimited power, is not given to you "carte blanche"; actual authority has to be acquired through your personality, expertise, work, performance, and honesty. Players are extremely smart, so you shouldn't ever underestimate them. They quickly assess and judge what kind of person you are. Are you someone credible, consistent, correct, fair, or honest? Only with truly built authority and trust, respect of the players can be gained. Players are wise and they differentiate between "coaches with authority" who are valued and respected, and "coaches who have power" who are not.

A coach with authority is followed out of respect, and the "powerful" coach is obeyed out of fear. To be respected and followed, you have to be able to solve their problems and potential conflicts that always might be experienced in some form in the team. Players expect you to be a good teacher of the game, someone who'll educate and inspire them.

The better you meet their expectations, the stronger your value will be in their eyes. The authority that is based on partnership and mutual respect between coach and player is long term. The key values of a coach in building this partnership with his players are fairness and honesty.

Should Players Like the Coach?

In terms of a coach's role, it's irrelevant whether the players like him or not. It's important that the coach adopts the correct attitude toward the players. Successful coaches have the highest regard for fairness, integrity, and achievement of common goals. On many occasions I've heard how various "do-gooders" tried to persuade the coach to make a move at the expense of others, which would increase his popularity and success. A coach should never allow himself to be persuaded to do this. The main criteria for doing certain things should always be its level of correctness and not a goal that can be achieved, regardless of increasing popularity or achieving sports success. Coaches who stick to these guidelines are respected by players and remain long in this ungrateful role. Therefore, in communication with the players, you have to adopt an attitude of truth and justice, because this is highly valued and respected among players. There'll always be those on the team who simply see themselves as "stars" and due to their talent they think they're above you and the other players. They even dare to criticize you and raise their voice in public. In such cases, you mustn't succumb to external pressures. A correct and honest approach to all your players and the public will secure your inner peace and allow a smooth operation without paying attention to this type of criticism. It feels good when players are influenced by their coach's procedures, which are in line with his words and his behavior. Successful coaches are unanimous in their attitude; the greatest success in sports is easiest to achieve with those who are modest and humble. Would Luka Modric, one of Real Madrid's flagship players, ever have unlocked his greatness if he hadn't been modest and humble in failure as well as in success?

The Captain Understands the Game and the Coach's Ideas

I'll explain why a successful coach always insists that the captain should be his choice. The team captain is the coach's right-hand man on the pitch. It's understandable that the captain can only be a person who enjoys the coach's unlimited trust. Equally, the captain needs to really understand the game and the coach's ideas. During the selection process, there mustn't be a false democracy and players must fully accept the coach's decision. It's crucial that the player has authority among the players and is a first team regular with a moral character. He also has to understand the game and know how to communicate. When selecting a captain, coaches are very demanding. They have to be, since the captaincy role is an essential link in the success of the team. The captain must lead his teammates in training and on match day. The captain has to know how the team is organized and its way of playing. Furthermore, the captain is the person who informs the coach about problems brewing in the team. The captain needs to assess which issues should be passed on to the coach, and he should know which challenges can be solved with a physical therapist or by the coach's assistants. The captaincy role among young players is priceless. The influence of the captain in developing the minds of young players can often be more useful than that of the actual coach. Only the captain can persuade young players that sacrifice is part and parcel of professional sport and without it there's no success. The coach should never set unrealistic objectives for the captain and players. If a coach's assessment suggests the team should reach seventh or eighth place, he should never force the captain and players to believe they could reach first or second place. At best, the coach must ignite the team's hope that eventually, at maximum effort and unity, they could fight for third or fourth place, which would lead to an international competition. The captain and the players may also assess the realistic possibilities of their own team although some coaches tend not to think so.

Team Success Without Prima Donnas

For any coach, the team selection is a complex and responsible task, something the coaches would know well themselves. The coach should never choose players who hold the exact same qualities as one another. The coach should choose players who are best suited to a particular position. The ideal choice for a coach is a combination of sports experts and uncompromising fighters: players with a strong character and athletic personalities. Naturally, it can't be the same to create a soccer team in Croatia, where players have enviable technical and tactical knowledge, as here in Ireland, where players' technical skills aren't so obvious. However, certain other qualities are more expressed, such as agility, speed, and a fighting spirit. And for sure in today's soccer the mastery of the ball is no longer enough to fight among the serious leagues. The complete player should possess technical and tactical knowledge along with a formed character, confidence, athletic qualities, work ethic, team mentality, and above all, a healthy lifestyle. The coach needs to explain to each player what his specific role in the team is and what's expected from him in order to be ready for all the challenges he faces during the season. Each player must be aware that the tasks given to him need to be achieved. If there's no one in the team who behaves like a prima donna, the team is destined for great success. If, however, there's such an individual in the team who only plays for himself, you can hardly expect a better result. Players who act in this way strive for self-promotion with their performance and attitude. The biggest problem for a coach with a prima donna attitude occurs when he doesn't do his job at the moment when the ball is lost. These kinds of players directly threaten the result of the team. In turn, his work has to be done by another player, which requires extra effort. Another problem for a coach with this type of player in his squad is the player's skills and creative lucidity, which often gains the sympathy of the public and the media. Many times I've witnessed matches where the behavior of the prima donna on the pitch, including self-promotion and doing things in his own way greatly contributed to the team's defeat. The only option to solve this situation is to talk to him in-depth and try to explain with a lot of empathy and understanding that what he's doing is harming himself and equally the team. You should constantly encourage him to change his approach to the game and motivate him to understand that playing for a team actually means playing for yourself. Converting an individual to a team player may take time and be bumpy along the way, but it's surely worth the effort as these individuals are, more or less, excellent soccer talents. The worst option is to leave him out of the team, as this leads to confrontation with the public and also the media, which is the last thing I want to happen to you.

Players Need to Know What Is Expected of Them

Every player should always know what's expected of him and what he can gain from the coach and his assistants. When meeting for the first time, the coach needs to explain to the players that the common goal of the team is always ahead of individual interest. So you should ask yourself how do you prepare your players before a game? Most coaches motivate players by giving them a speech, yet equally, there are plenty of coaches who tend to provide an overview of expectations and detailed information about the next opponent in writing. I prefer coaches who give a short, stimulating and encouraging speech before a match. In my opinion, a dull piece of paper, no matter how much relevant information it contains, can't replace the personal contact and emotion that coaches convey to their players. I say this as primarily the coach has plenty of time during week-long preparations before the match to inform players about important details relating to the game and the opponent. I like the philosophy of the wise Chinese Sun in which commanders of the army, and that's exactly what coaches are, should always aim to beat the opponent before the match begins. In order to succeed you need studious preparation, good knowl-edge of your opponent, and a lot of tactical exercises and meetings with your players. The entire week before the game, coaches have to work on the preparation and motivation of the players for the upcoming match. Based on this, the players should know the prepared strategy on the day of the match by heart and would be ready for every possible situation and surprise. After preparations for the match are complete, every other form of motivation, apart from a brief speech on the eve of the match would seem counterproductive and would probably make players feel tense. During preparations, a successful coach never humiliates his rivals or their coaches and players. He equally treats his players in the same way. In addition to the team as a whole, during the week he endeavors to motivate each individual player. Young players shouldn't need to be particularly motivated as they are really eager to prove themselves and anxious to take advantage of the opportunity.

Notice Your Players and See the Rewards

During the competitive season, coaches are usually more concerned with how players perform their tactical tasks than the team results. To be able to do that, a sense of peace and harmony in the team is needed. Every time you have the opportunity, try to isolate yourself from external influences. Players know how to relax, especially the younger ones, so they constantly need to be encouraged and motivated to work hard. They need to be motivated to follow instructions as this leads to the perfection of performance to achieve the desired game. To be able to do that, you have to get each player to understand that he plays an important role in achieving the common goal. Lots of conversations, praise, and a positive approach always create good results. When the players are convinced that you notice them, that you appreciate their hard work and dedication, they'll give their best in training and matches. Players shouldn't only be encouraged to develop their sports skills. At least once a week you should work with them on developing their emotional and social skills. When I worked in the professional soccer club in Croatia, our key player, a midfielder, used to be distracted at every home match by the abusive comments shouted from the crowds, which affected his play. Our head coach talked to him about it during each preparation, drawing his attention to focus only on the game and not to be distracted by the shouts from the fans. Before an important match, during his motivational speech for the game, our coach would hang a large picture of a cat chasing a mouse in the dressing room. He did this to explain to players that the cat doesn't think about whether someone is watching while hunting the mouse. The cat is completely focused on how to catch its prey—the little mouse.

It reacts by instinct. That's a reaction he looked for from the players—to behave like cats in a game. He asked them to fully focus on the game to bring us victory and not the screaming comments from the crowd, or the wrong decisions of the referee. When he motivated them to behave like a cat, he actually asked players to go through the match with a hunter's instinct. This went down really well with the players. That type of motivation, given through a story, proved to be very encouraging and built a positive team spirit. The higher the frequency of praise and encouragement on coach's part, the better the positive atmosphere in the team. Our coach also noticed when it comes to younger players, it's better to praise their performance immediately after an exercise than at a meeting after training. Compliments are very encouraging, but they must never be given without reason. They should be only given when truly deserved. The same goes for criticism. When players are ineffective in their performance, show understanding for this, but also point out the mistake and give them a solution for it. All players have their bad days and they'll appreciate it when their coach shows understanding and not an immediate lesson because of a poor performance.

Players Cannot Be Guided on the Basis of Praise Alone

It's quite normal for experienced coaches to accept that players need to relax from time to time and the fact that sometimes they can get up to mischief. It's human and natural. Most young men, at some point during their youth, are unable to resist life's naughty temptations and go off the rails in their behavior. There are usually two tactics successful coaches use when faced with behavioral issues from the players. One is used in mild circumstances. It consists of complete ignorance or disregard to the inappropriate behavior of the player. Coaching practice has shown that this behavior of the players, if simply ignored by the coach, eventually fades away and disappears. Another tactic is applied when the player's behavior has put themselves or others at risk, or when they disturb the team activities and tarnish the reputation of the club. In this case, the coach should immediately react. In private, the player in question should be informed such behavior will not be tolerated and must stop instantly, otherwise punishment will follow. This attitude should be consistent, which means that the coach is willing to drop such a player from the team or even club, regardless of his status and previous performance on the pitch. However, penalizing players should only be undertaken if that's what you're really forced to do. But once you've decided to go for it, it should be carried out properly and effectively. You have to accept it's impossible to lead the players only on the basis of praise or expectations and that inappropriate behavior will simply disappear by itself. I once knew a coach who used to punish his player's behavior by getting them to sing in a public place chosen by the coach. As a young coach he was ambitious and would financially penalize players for each offence. After some time he realized that he was always trying to punish the behavior of the same player and that he wasn't using the same disciplinary measures for the entire team. In contrast, the singing punishment proved to be very effective. This was confirmed by one of his players who had to sing in front of two hundred guests during preseason training in Spain.

Respect Your Players

Today coaches are often evaluated through the prism of their material achievement, the home they live in, or the watch they wear. Even the car they drive could be a means of assessing their performance. Qualities such as expertise, sports results, honesty, wisdom, and respect are often neglected. I wonder where did the basic human values that we were raised on and taught by our parents disappear? Respect has gone. Are China, America, and Japan the only places on earth left where the coach or teacher is actually respected? Despite all of this, I don't want to believe that the reality is so dark and gloomy. The most effective way of gaining respect in the coaching profession is when the coach himself shows interest and a positive attitude toward players and coworkers, toward their feelings, attitudes, and habits. A successful coach respects his players, colleagues, and coworkers, takes care of them, and encourages them to progress. How many times have we tried to stop somebody talking because we didn't agree with them? How many times have we criticized players for a "wrong" move? How often have we shared advice even without being asked? Respect players, always make the first move to solve a dispute, let journalists freely express their opinions, praise the environment in which you perform, and you'll be a successful coach. The role of a coach is becoming increasingly demanding day by day. Coaches are constantly expected to do more and better themselves. One doesn't have to be too wise to notice that mutual respect within the team develops a general respect for the club, including the management, sponsors, and officials. The way players treat you, their attitude toward the club and training with respect, or lack of it, depends on how much respect they previously developed growing up at home. It also certainly depends on the amount of respect you're willing to show them as a coach. Every coach should be aware of this! It's immensely important that coaches accept the share of responsibility in how players behave. As a role model, the coach certainly affects the way his players behave. Does their behavior fit into the communication etiquette of the civilized club? There are so many more elements, along with respect that are necessary and important to be a successful coach. The coach himself is the one who should be able to recognize the importance of all elements affecting his coaching success. Teaching sports skills requires broad expertise, which has to be continually supplemented with additional education. Players always expect positive impetus from the coach.

Players are the ones who use the coaches' expertise and experience to realize their sporting goals. The opinion of the coach is often a critical stance for most players. Players need respect from the coach and his support. I don't know a single case where a player succeeded without the support of a coach and if there is one, it's a rare thing. Not a single player will succeed without a good teacher. If the coach doesn't respect the players, players won't respect him either. If the coach has a negative attitude about everything, everyone around him will become a loser. Good always attracts good!

How to "Strip Down" the Players

Have you ever been taught statistics in school? I was taught in school that statistics is an element of applied mathematics that deals with the collection, processing, interpretation, and presentation of data. Statistics wasn't exactly my favorite subject at school and I never would have imagined my friends as sports coaches would use them with so much enthusiasm. Statistics has become a critical tool for coaches in making crucial decisions. Thanks to statistics, coaches know how far players run, how many passes they make, and how many of them are complete or incomplete. Just as a high jumper knows the exact height he jumped, coaches also have very precisely measured indicators of player performance. Today, thanks to the sophisticated tracking system, using cameras installed at the stadium, it's possible to gain extremely useful data that provides your professional team real insight into the physical and technical possibilities of individual players and the entire team. With the results that can be obtained, coaches today can completely "strip down" players to basic statistical analysis—meters run, fouls made, accuracy of passes, and so on. Statistics help the coach and club management, but also journalists, to be more objective in giving an assessment of somebody's performance. Without these exact indicators it certainly wouldn't be possible to do that. The great thing about the power of statistics is that everyone who doesn't understand the game can understand statistical indicators pretty well. Regardless of the exact indicators obtained, the overall performance of players during a game is immeasurable as the statistical indicators are used more to "strip down" the players.

Accelerate the Recovery of Players

Can you imagine any expert team in sports without the doctor? Today, without working with a medical expert, it's practically impossible to achieve good results. Although the most common public perception is that the primary role of the physician is to treat and rehabilitate athletes, this is only partly true. In addition to the ongoing concern of the treatment and rehabilitation of athletes, he or she plays an essential role in the field of nutrition and monitoring the training process. The physician himself, without cooperation from the coach, simply wouldn't be able to protect athletes from injuries. Cooperation from the coach is essential, as it's important a coach has at least a basic understanding of sports medicine and recognizes the scope of a doctor's work in the team. Muscle analysis is crucial in preventing athletes from getting injured. Players coached by my friends, Croatian coaches, knew in advance that at the beginning of each season certain measurements of muscle strength were to be achieved. After the experts performed detailed analysis of muscle groups of each player and later on through the training process, any deficiencies identified during testing were corrected through individual work. Cooperation with the doctor proves to be essential in assessing the ability of an injured athlete. As coaches try to accelerate the recovery of athletes and their return to the pitch, doctors are always skeptical, convinced that returning is premature. I noticed regardless of how much the injured player is essential to the team, you always hand the final decision to the doctor and his ethics, which oblige him not to allow an insufficiently recovered player back on the pitch. Although I must say there have been cases, when the club doctor accepted the risk, at the cost of reinjury. Coaches and doctors must also cooperate in the fight against the use of banned substances through continuous education and the constant philosophy that these drugs are detrimental to their health. And finally, sports success can never be more important than human health.

Right Food Leads to High Performance

Sweetgreen is my favorite when it comes to healthy food. I just love their guacamole greens salads. A healthy diet is extremely important for the players, because it helps optimal development, good concentration, and increases durability and resistance. Science has proved that the basic processes of releasing energy needed for intense physical effort are directly related to the quantity and quality of a player's diet. The daily balanced diet of players should be rich in vitamins, minerals, and other nutritional substances. In sports nutrition, an adequate intake of proteins that build muscles and carbohydrates filling the energy reserve readily available in the body is extremely important. The consumption of vitamins and minerals is increased for players. These must be taken in the form of rich foods or supplements. Athletes should eat as much fresh, natural food as they can find. Thanks to spending time with players for many years, I've noticed that players who eat proper foods can maintain a high training intensity, recover faster from injuries, and achieve better results. When we talk about the importance of nutrition for the players, the importance of water intake is often neglected. Water is particularly important for a player's body. Players consume large quantities during training and matches. The body needs to compensate for the fluids lost through sweating because even a low dehydration of 2 percent can significantly reduce the effect of a player in a game (www.ncbi.nlm.nih.gov).

Regarding the most suitable diet for a player, coaches should consult a doctor and a nutritionist. The operational process of ordering and controlling the food for the players in restaurants should be left to the club's physiotherapist. In addition to the recommendations of doctors and nutritionists in relation to the right diet, coaches can also rely on their own experience or the experience of those he trusts. An interesting example is a personal approach to diet by Croatian coach Zlatko Ivankovic, who insists on a large consumption of honey in his players' diets. When I discussed this with him, I learned that he insists on the highest possible consumption of natural honey due to the high content of vitamins and minerals. The content of protein, amino acids, and enzymes gives honey added value because this is great for cell regeneration after intensive training. Along with this, honey is rich in essential amino acids that the human body can't produce, so it must be taken with food.

Let's Give the Players What They Want

There's only one way to motivate players. The only way you can influence players to assure maximum commitment to football and the training sessions is to give them what they want. And what exactly do they want? Almost every player wants to achieve a successful playing career, to play for a big club, and to be important and appreciated. Every player wants to express his creativity and personality to the maximum. And in reality not many of them are thinking about their health, family, and the future. All of them first of all want to be recognized and respected in their environment. A coach who manages to deepen the sense of personal importance in a player will turn him into a friend and those who don't comply usually face difficulties in communication with other players. Try, therefore, to deepen the sense of personal importance in each of the players. It's nothing new or unknown. Feeling recognized and respected is one of the most important needs of every human being. Every player craves for the approval of those who they're in contact with. They all want their efforts and their true value recognized among those who follow sport. Every player genuinely cares about recognition from the public. How can you persuade players to give maximum effort during training and on the pitch?

Only when you manage to create a good relationship with the players and a strong spirit among the players will you be able to ignite their enthusiasm and inspire what's most valuable to them. Experience has taught me that there's nothing as disastrous for the player's will and ego as criticism from the coach. Criticizing and belittling the players is not effective. Far more can be achieved by showing encouragement and sharing praise. Genuine praise is the recipe for successful communication with the players. In giving praise and credit to players, a coach can always show his honesty. I know certain coaches who have a habit of flattering players. Flattery rarely achieves anything with players as they can spot exactly what's genuine and what isn't. Mere flattery is doomed to fail, although unfortunately there are some players who crave for recognition and enjoy it even if they don't deserve it. This also applies to certain coaches: "Don't be afraid of the enemy who attacks you, but rather the friend who flatters you."

How to Get Players to Listen to Your Advice

Many coaches make mistakes as they want players to buy into their views at all costs. No one likes to listen to advice and instructions, not even the players. We would all prefer to work according to our conscience and feel that our decisions are respected and praised. Players prefer when coaches respect them as a person, when they're asked about their hopes and when their work and effort is respected. When I was living and working in Croatia, I spent a lot of time talking with Croatian soccer coaches. In addition to talking about already mentioned topics, we would often go back in time remembering our former coaches and their styles of training. We remembered one particular late Croatian coach, who coached us when we were just young lads. He was a gentleman and a great pedagogue, who never gave direct commands. He would never say to players "do this and that!" or "don't do this and that!" The instructions from our favorite coach were always given in the form of advice and suggestions such as "I suggest you do this," "maybe you could try it another way!" Only today, and that's a good 30 years later, can I realistically perceive the quality and greatness of his communication. With such a distinctive way of communication, he was building our self-criticism as young players and encouraging us to train hard and cooperate with others. It's an interesting question to ask why today's modern coaches don't act in the same way.

A Successful Coach Embraces His Own Weaknesses

Life's rapid pace and the daily struggle to achieve objectives don't leave much time for coaches themselves and their personal development. Despite this, every coach should find time to devote to himself. Every coach should look internally at himself as much as possible. Success in life depends not so much on how hard you work, but on how well you think. Respecting yourself and others, being self-critical, listening to others, and understanding and admitting your mistakes are requirements that a man needs to meet at the very start in order to become a fulfilled and mature person. So everyone should ask themselves whether you have ever made efforts to live a peaceful, fulfilled, and happy life?

Only spiritual development can truly bring people joy and happiness. Spiritual development builds a positive attitude not only within yourself, but also to the surrounding environment. A happy and fulfilled man can only become one who is ready to embrace his weaknesses, the one who learns from his mistakes and the one who recognizes his qualities and uses them to his advantage. Great is the one who, in addition to admitting them, has the courage to resolve his own problems. Such people are happy and successful, as their mental state and perspectives don't depend on others.

In Life No Effort Is Wasted

"What are the most important qualities needed to achieve coaching success?" There are many people who have asked me this question. In fact, this is what all young coaches ask. Although they all, considering my age and experience, expect some sort of great wisdom from me, I'll probably disappoint them with a simple and humble answer: an immense love for people and for sports, many painstaking hours of hard work and perseverance. In this I always emphasize that no effort in life is in vain. Every effort, however, even the smallest, is always worth it, and it's always fertilized in some form, either materially or spiritually. If you love something enthusiastically, if you give your all and trust everything inside of you to become something good and positive, nothing will prevent you from achieving your set goal. The truth is there'll always be thorns and roses along the way to the finish line, but it's fully worth the effort and worth a try. Be persistent, constantly absorb new knowledge, and develop yourself because this is the only way to reach the results you want. Young coaches are impatient and often find it a challenge to work as an assistant, with ideas of immediately becoming a head coach. Young coaches should be taught from the very beginning of their coaching career that this is a big mistake which they'll only realize later in their profession. Sometimes a young coach can be faced with a great opportunity and can even experience a sudden success, but without the necessary experience this success can quickly turn from a "flash-in-the-pan" to the "bubble being burst". And the journey from then on can be very difficult and painful, and often impossible. The road to coaching success is not an overnight journey from victory to defeat, it's a long-term process; it's a marathon, not a sprint. It's a route with many stops along the way and with constant checks. These constant evaluation points are the best motivation boosters to achieve continuous future success measured by results. Coaches are constantly put in risky situations accepting a variety of challenges. The challenges force them to constantly invest in themselves, either through additional professional education, or through working on themselves in order to strengthen self-control and concentration. Coaches are actually eternally addicted to objectives and challenges and all of us working in sports are like that. I simply can't imagine life without goals or challenges. Challenges are by far my best fix, filling me with adrenaline, forcing me to give my best and grab them with both hands.

The Difficulties in Achieving a Successful Coaching Career

What's the reason why so many former players, who were successful in their playing careers, did not achieve a similar success as a coach?

A successful coaching career is difficult to achieve because of the many characteristics coaches need to have. It's merely not enough to possess the basic elements that all former great players undoubtedly have, such as certain sports knowledge and experience. Other characteristics and skills of the individual are crucial, namely intelligence, character, effective communication, and attitude. There's also courage, responsibility, self-control, a teamwork ethic, and hard work. Many of athletes I know had a previous career as a great soccer players, and that started them off with a great advantage. The charisma they had was the key that opened the door to every club, but to their regret that same key didn't unlock the door to their coaching greatness. The glorious playing career and coaching talent are not enough to control various personal issues some coaches have, such as drinking, gambling, or similar. If you take a closer look, you can easily discover the majority of former top players who had successful soccer playing careers fail over time as a coach, with honorable exceptions such as Jupp Heynckes and Carlo Ancelotti. The best example of this is Diego Maradona, one of the best players in the history of soccer.

The majority of former top players are convinced that the mere fact that they were top football players is enough to position them at the very top in the coaching profession. Only hard-working, persevering coaches with human virtues, fully dedicated to the team on a daily basis, can achieve a successful coaching career. Believe me, a coach can't be successful if he has a vice, such as gambling, betting, or alcohol.

What Does Success Mean?

Each of us wants to be successful in the job we do. Since the beginning of mankind, man has been constantly striving for something better, more beautiful, and more perfect. The same applies to sports coaches. Coaches are constantly striving for something better and bigger. Whether it's about the players, results, clubs, or money, they always strive for more. In the club I used to work for, I've seen a dozen senior team coaches come and go. The most successful were those who, apart from knowing their job, were aware that the key to success is in themselves. What we are depends on what we think. Each investment in the fundamental principles of success, honesty and perseverance will always be more than repaid. In an effort to create a high-quality relationship with the players, management, and the media, successful coaches can often change their attitudes and way of working. If we're not willing to change, it's highly possible we've reached our maximum potential. For years I've watched many of successful coaches, changing their attitude and behavior during their stay at the club in order to get the maximum from the players, compared with others who have insisted on the players changing themselves in order to adapt to them. No change is easy, but with strong faith, a great desire and perseverance, anything can be achieved. And if you lose a match, which will happen for sure, you don't have to worry about defeat, as victory and defeat are an integral part of the coaching job. Moreover, defeat doesn't even have to be a mistake; it can sometimes be the best thing to happen to a coach at just the right time. You have to learn to accept defeat but only temporarily. There is a beautiful saying: "Failures are the steps to success." There's not one coach who hasn't faced painful defeats and failures at the beginning of his career. It takes time until they realize that failure is just part of the lessons that lead them to success. Your latest defeat, although it may seem at this point so painful, even though it wasn't your first, won't be your last either.

You might wonder if the fear you felt before the match was the reason for defeat? Would the soccer team of my small, recently established Croatia have ever won second place at the World Cup in Russia in 2018 if the coach Zlatko Dalic was afraid of failure? Failure is an integral part of the pathway in life that everybody must walk along. The more spiritual and more persistent we become, the less failure and more success to follow there will be. If you consider your coaching role as a reflection of fulfillment, respect, focus, and an immense love for the sport, you'll achieve success in your coaching career, regardless of the results.

I've Always Stood Up for What Burns Inside Me

Most of the public who follow sports consider coaches as very sociable people. People who are never alone, always surrounded by others. Is this just an illusion or is this the reality? If you would ask any coach he would assure you that this is a mere illusion. Interestingly, the role of a coach is actually quite lonely. Coaches are mostly self-denying people who always open new roads, perceive new opportunities when others fail to notice them and enjoy being alone deep within their thoughts. They're always thinking two steps ahead. And because of this they're often misunderstood and criticized. How to resist it? We shouldn't resist. We just have to be ourselves. The coach needs to tap into all of the resources and means he can think of to impose his attitude. A successful coach won't accept nor support anything that seems mediocre. A successful coach always stands up for what burns inside of him. With all due respect, every coach should listen to other people's opinions and advice, but accept and take on board only what contributes to his vision of excellence. The game of soccer not only requires the good physical condition of players, but also the willingness of their heart and mind. Sometimes players are in excellent physical shape, but their heart is far from ready. Have you ever found yourself in a situation when your mind wants to take control of your body, but the body refuses to cooperate? In football it's the same as in life. All "family members"—the body, mind, and heart—have to work together. The game will never be complete if even only one member, either body, mind, or heart, doesn't participate in the game.

The Philosophy of Coaching as Part of the Family

There is a saying that behind every successful man there's a woman, and vice versa. Also, behind every successful coach there's his coaching philosophy. This term refers to how coaches perceive players and in turn create relationships with them. After so many years of friendship and spending time with coaches, I noticed that all of them perceive the philosophy of the coaching experience as if it's an integral part of their family. This doesn't surprise me, as they've shaped, built and grown with it, the same way as they've built their family over the years. And they usually have also incorporated much of their own temperament and character into their coaching philosophy. There's no successful philosophy or superior results without enthusiasm and passion. Each coaching philosophy has its own distinctive handwriting. Coaching philosophy isn't created, as some people simplify it, from game to game or from victory to defeat. It's built and matured over many years. The creation of the coaching philosophy is influenced by education, family, and the environment in which you were raised. It also consists of a great deal of published words and generally accepted beliefs that you've read in books or heard on television, building up over the years into a library or database in your head. As someone who's familiar with the coaching style of my friends, Branko Ivankovic and Drazen Besek, Croatian soccer coaches who have worked in China, I recognize the great impact of China's spiritual way of thinking in their coaching philosophy. Initially, I recognized the ideology they adopted from the great Chinese teacher Sun Tzu, author of one of the world's best-selling books *The Art of War*. Sun Tzu's thoughts aren't what the book's title might suggest, only applicable to the military aspects of human activity. The fundamental philosophical ideas from the book, such as victory over the enemy before the fight, my coaching friends now apply to their coaching. Their philosophy of coaching equals their perspective on life which has been shaped over time. It's a guideline that determines the methods of their work, their relationships with the players and how to form a game. Every coach should read this book. As a young coach building your own coaching philosophy, you mustn't forget to include your personality in forming your own philosophy of coaching, regardless of the fact that your coaching role and your behavior will be considerably influenced by your set goals.

Think Positively and See How Your Life Changes

Have you noticed that there are lots of coaches who constantly have something to complain about? They complain about the referees and officials, the players, the management, the media, or low wages. For so many coaches, moaning and regret is a common characteristic and even after a string of sporting successes or a strong financial deal, they simply can't hide their dissatisfaction. Surely, this isn't healthy. The constant gloom does nothing but enhance the negativity even further, creating a vicious circle. There isn't one coach who has ever strengthened his position by complaining about the players, referees, management, fans, or the media. Contrary to the plan, this would only inflame the anger making things worse. I once knew a coach who would forever blame the referee for the defeat. Not only did he fail to gain anything from his negative comments, the only thing he did manage to ever gain was damage. His referee complaints provoked ridicule among the sporting public, which interpreted his actions as a search for an excuse for his team's defeat. Having a negative approach to all aspects of coaching can do a lot of damage to the coaches as their attention diverts from the good things that are happening to them at work. A coach, who possesses an already embedded negative attitude, will hinder his own chances of happiness and enjoying the beautiful game. On the contrary there are coaches who switch things around, nurturing a positive attitude. Their view of the world around them is positive and I'm sure that a positive attitude and appreciation for this influences the quality of their life. In sports there have and always will be situations where it's difficult to adopt a positive mind-set. What positives can be found in a situation where you've been severely betrayed by the referee, when he unfairly turns the game in favor of your rival? A positive attitude doesn't mean to mislead or ignore the facts, but regardless of the circumstances, we can again choose to be positive or negative. We make a choice. It's certainly easier to get into a negative frame of mind, than a positive one. How can we avoid a negative attitude? Just like most things in life, a positive attitude and gratitude can be learned by practice. Positive thinking should be exercised. For me, the best exercise is when I'm in bed just before going to sleep. I go through the day in my mind and focus on the good things that have happened and number all the things I can be thankful for. There are certain days when I can't think of many good things but I always manage to find at least one good thing, a person that I like or something good that has happened to me and I think about it evoking the most beautiful memories and pictures. Every time I think about someone negatively, I immediately remind myself that this person must have at least five times more positive qualities. I just haven't noticed them. Since cultivating an attitude of gratitude and positivity, the quality of my life has improved. It really has. I feel happier and more complete.

The World Appreciates Success, Not Value

There is a common opinion among coaches that the most important skill to achieve success in the coaching profession is to be a good teacher and educator and to have knowledge about theory and practice of technique, tactic, and condition training.

Well, I will convince you, by using arguments, that the above findings are no longer sufficient to achieve a successful coaching career.

Why? Because today, the presentation of the coach himself and presentation of his professional coaching experience is just as important, if not even more important than his expertise and results. Today a coach needs to be popular and has to have positive image beside his expert knowledge and sports results. And the popularity can be gained only if his professional work, experience, and sports results are adequately promoted. If so, the sympathy is won and emotions among sports public caught. The more emotions evoked in public, the more chances to gain sympathy and create a positive image in public.

In order to successfully present himself and his expertise, the coach has to have at least basic knowledge about sports marketing and communication skills. If the coach is not able to successfully present himself and his knowledge, the result is usually missing.

The Success and Happiness of a Coach Depends Not Only on Knowledge but Also on the Virtues

Have you ever wondered why some coaches have the power, success, and happiness in their profession, and the others don't, although they have the same level of education and they've graduated at the same schools?

Because success and happiness depend not only on knowledge but also on virtues. Knowledge, talent, skill, and technology are a help, and virtues are power.

We all notice the qualities of a coach who is a team worker, a good communicator, and a motivator. A coach using the aforementioned features shows that he acquired these, for his job significant skills, through education, training, or additional training.

But what about at first glance hidden, "intangible" but powerful elements of the coach's personality that are called the virtues? Virtues cannot be adopted the same way as skills can, they are determined through experience and beliefs in their key role in achieving personal happiness and success.

The virtues are the key element to distinguish good from top coaches. If the coach possesses virtues such as honesty, perseverance, consistency, authenticity, patience, curiosity, athletes and the sporting public are able to follow him obediently.

I know there are many who will say but we live in times and in the environment that first of all appreciates the skills. Coaches who know how to communicate, and smile when it's needed or not, right?

Regardless of the current "populist" times and the popularity of such coaches, it is about short-term "players" that will be forgotten the moment they are replaced by their sports organization. And in contrast, there are coaches who, apart from adopting skills mentioned above, possess the virtues. They will be mentioned in the clubs and among the athletes even then when they will no longer be there. Because they possess the virtues that elevate them and make them beautiful, so they leave a positive trace in their actions.

One of the most important virtues of a coach is honesty. There is a reason to say that honesty is more valuable than diamonds. The honesty of a coach in sports is not familiar to any resort to cheating. Honor in sports implies fidelity to commitments, humility in victory, generosity to the defeated, patience with spectators who are not always moderate, fairness if competitive sport is associated with financial contractual interests (Pius XII 2002, http://abbeyathletics.com). The first ones who feel the coach's dishonesty are athletes, as their wakeful eye can not miss it.

The next virtue that leads to coach's success is perseverance. The persistent coaches do not overlook the problems they are facing; they are being solved as they come up. They do not give up in accomplishing the set goals after the first defeat, or after comments by unsatisfied fans and media. They are persistent in the intent of implementing their ideas, knowing that defeats are an integral part of their work. They are determined; decisions are made in due time after a detailed "for and against" analysis, and when they decide for something, that decision usually stays.

Some coaches are nervous because the players do not listen to them, especially those who work with children. "Do not worry that children never listen to you; worry that they are always watching you" (http://www.cpsetanta.ie).

This often cited statement by American writer Robert Fulghum who tells us that the point of work with children, in our case with athletes, is in the consistency of what we are saying, how we are acting, and how this is implemented in our work. Beside parents, coaches are the most important persons for athletes, so their behavior and action are absorbed like a sponge. Coaches often underestimate the importance of their exposure to observation and constant scrutiny by athletes. As watchful observers, the athletes can very quick evaluate the (non)virtues of their coach and determine whether he is credible, persistent in the values he represents, and loyal and dedicated to the common goals. If the coach firmly holds the values he narrates and advocates, the athletes can see it very well. Finally, watching the coach, athletes might conclude that the goals he represent are not worth the effort or that they are worthy to fight and sacrifice for them.

CHAPTER 6

What Is the Future of Sports Business?

Is the growth of successful sports organizations sustainable in the face of ever more pronounced technological revolutions and political uncertainties?

To keep up the growth of sports industry, it is crucial for people who work in sports to have a vision of how the Internet will change the sport. Because what 10 years ago seemed unthinkable is today's reality. Sports industry must compete with people playing football, soccer, basketball, and baseball online. Sports arenas are increasingly replaced by mobile phones and laptops screens.

The e-sport industry behind it has another record growth year. Competitive gaming in the mentioned competition systems for a particular audience has been fairly steeped in the mainstream and has shown its full potential to the world. From hobbies and entertainment, it has become a future leisure industry with endless possibilities.

Traditional revenue generated from ticket sales has been lagging behind in the race with new technologies for a long time now. It is also evident that the days of watching free sports through the TV are counted, and that watching sports will be charged over TV or online on demand. The 21st century sports will continue to focus more on the players like Amazon, Apple, and Google in order to keep up the growth, rather than a development of existing TV media.

What Can Be Expected from Sports in the 21st Century?

Is it possible to maintain the growth of sports industry in the shadow of marked technological revolution and political uncertainties?

I suppose that in the future, in sport, the least changes will happen in the classical, competitive part of it because it has always been quite conservative. In all other parts of sports and around sports, there will be changes and they will be fascinating. To be able to deal better with the changes, the people working in sport have to understand in what way the progress of technology and the Internet will change sport. The continuous growth of the sports industry can be maintained only by focusing on future and timely reaction to questions and opportunities that will affect the sports industry in the coming years.

The ticket sales, which use to represent a basic source of income for sports organizations, have for a long time now no primacy over revenue. It is also evident that the days of watching free sports through the TV are counted, and that watching sports will be charged over TV or online "on demand." The 21st century sports will, instead of holding on to existing TV media, continue to hold on to the new big players such as Amazon, Apple, and Google, to keep pace with growth and development. The new technologies are winning the sports industry step by step.

In the upcoming period, the sports organization will have a tough job to take fans out of their cosy homes to a live event, using a variety of benefits and entertainment. Fans who have traditionally bought tickets for a live event expect more flexibility from sporting organizations and more content. There are already some positive examples:

In an attempt to cater to a more diverse set of fans, organizations like the New York Jets have rolled out subscription-based mobile passes that allow fans to attend a predetermined number of games for a flat fee. Through these subscriptions, seat location varies depending on ticket availability, which allows for fans to have a unique experience at each game. In other cases, organizations like the New Jersey Devils are offering a "banking" system membership, whereby fans choose to make an advance deposit into an account, which is debited to purchase tickets throughout the season. By offering the ability of choosing from any game and any ticket quantity at discounted prices, fans are given the flexibility that more traditional season-ticket packages don't often provide (www2.deloitte.com).

Over the last few years, we have witnessed the disappearance of cable television and the proliferation of new smart services delivered by the new technology. In the same way that changes are accepted by viewers in the media industry, the shift in accepting changes can be noticed both in sports organizations and sports brands. One way, classical mass marketing that promotes sports events on billboards and through TV ads is slowly disappearing. Instead, advertising costs are shifted to digital means and social networks, because using them the sports organizations and sports brands can more effectively target fans who are interested in their content.

E-Sport Is the Future of the Entertainment Industry

It seemed unthinkable to us a decade ago that sport would have to compete with people playing online football, soccer, basketball, and today this has become normal. Sports arenas are increasingly replaced by screens. Over the last few years we have witnessed a huge growth in the popularity and relevance of e-sports. Just like all the sports we're used to watching, e-sport is regularly taking place as part of fairly well-organized competitions, and the biggest professionals are superstars as well as the rest of the sports society, which can be seen on lawns, parquets, and paths.

You've probably had the chance to read about some of the new kids who make big money playing fun games. It's not about stereotypes of kids we see in movies and series. And neither about the big kids who are sitting in front of the computer and play games, tapping into chips on the table. These "kids" spin our annual incomes, and the top players among them, make even multiyear wages in one match and have sponsorship contracts. Although the e-sport is in full swing, the time of its full flourishing is just about to come. E-sport has some touch points with the sport, but there is also a big difference. In the traditional sport fans are divided between teams and in e-sport, they are part of the gaming community and their competitions remind more of a festival. The e-sport is first for the game fan, and only then for the team playing the game.

What are e-sports?

The term e-sports refers to organized competitive gaming among professional players. Although there are many games that can be included in the space, the most popular games are generally team-based multiplayer games from the first-person shooter or multiplayer online battle arena genre. The audience can watch the event by either visiting the arena live or online through gaming broadcasters (www.forbes.com). Although the earliest known video game competition took place in 1972, the growth of e-sports really began in the early 1990s, as many games began to benefit from increased Internet connectivity and online play (www.valuewalk.com).

What contributes to e-sports revenue?

Per Newzoo, e-sports revenue is comprised of the components listed below. Sponsorships are the largest contributor. Until now, sponsorships have been largely driven by tech companies such as Intel, or gaming peripheral companies such as SteelSeries. Advertising is the second largest contributor. Major players in the advertising space for e-sports include computer components manufacturers and energy drinks, especially Red Bull. Media rights revenues are the revenues paid by broadcasting partners who own the rights to broadcast live games. Twitch and YouTube gaming are two major players in this space (www.forbes.com).

E-sport will soon become a major competitor to a classical sports business. The interest in this new form of sport is most commonly shown by the youngest users who are mostly recreational players themselves, but they are not the only ones because the most successful players are most often in their 20s and 30s.

When e-sport began to expand expeditiously, many realized that one of the key segments that must be improved is the mode of broadcasting of matches and tournaments. The first adjustments went through the games themselves, and later the work in production also followed.

There is even now an e-League, organized competitions that are transmitted on YouTube and Twitch.tv as well on some TV channels, such as TBS. From the very beginning, on entering the world of e-sports, e-League has set standards for the transfer of its own competitions, which is understandable given that behind the project there is the American media conglomerate Turner Broadcasting System. In order for the entire project to be successful, they brought in people with the necessary knowledge and invested in the studio for which they were awarded with an Emmy award (https://blitzesports.com).

The e-sports industry has grown at a tremendous pace over the past few years. According to a report from Newzoo, total e-sports revenue jumped from $493 million in 2016 to $655 million in 2017, and total revenue could exceed $900 million in 2018 (www.forbes.com).

The Coaching Profession Tomorrow?

We walked up the second staircase of the 21st century. Mechanical technology has been replaced with the digital one, forest and athletic tracks have been replaced by treadmills, and baseball, soccer, and basketball by digital games? Sport has become a business where the stakes are high as well as risks, especially at the elite level. The goal of a coach's career is no longer security, but personal and professional growth. Commercialization of sports is reflected in the evolution of the role of a coach. Today in sport there is a highlight on the personality of the actors, and impression is created that the fate of a sports organization or athlete is the sole responsibility of a coach, which certainly does not match the truth. However, athletes are the ones who score, break the records, settle the matches, and their quality and progress depend largely on the financial situation in a sports organization. Coaches tomorrow will not be protected from the real life that includes irrational and emotional condemnations of the sports public. Coaches can only fight against the continuous pressures of the public with constant education and redistribution of part of their work to their associates. Inevitably, there will be changes in the national structure of the players, who will be coached. In such conditions, a coach can achieve a successful career only through continuous education, and using advanced communication skills in order to match the differences of players with regard to education, preference, and religion. It is certain that the aforementioned differences will encourage coaches to enrich their knowledge of the languages, culture, religion, and different habits and ways of life that will be brought in from the players from different continents.

Because of the enhanced sports promotion in the society, the coaches will also have to face the influence of rich and popular players, which, given their significance, financial situation, and media popularity will be supported by the ownership structure of sports organizations. Changes will also happen because of the necessity of increased fitness preparations and loads of players due to the increasing number of official competitions.

The question of the moment is when it will happen that the players look fresh at the end of the competition just like at the beginning, thanks to various breathing techniques and accelerated recovery. We are fortunate that the technique and the medicine still have no impact on our heads, our attitudes, and reactions. We can only influence our thoughts and feelings ourselves. The art of thinking management is for now an invisible and unattainable world for the science. Its forces are powerful, and it is on each one of us to discover and use them. When found, it means the solution for all problems burdening us has been found.

References

Aaker, D.A., and M.B. Equity. 1991. The Free Press, New York, NY.

abbeyathletics.com, 2018. "Pope Pius XII Quote on Sport Properly Directed." from https://abbeyathletics.prestosports.com//sport_virtue/pope_pius_xii_quote_on_sport_proprely_directed

Badenhausen, K. 2018. "The World's Most Valuable Brands 2018." from https://forbes.com/sites/kurtbadenhausen/2018/05/23/the-worlds-most-valuable-brands-2018/#7a0e480d610c

Bauer, H.H., N.E. Stokburger-Sauer, and S. Exler. 2008. "Brand Image and Fan Loyalty in Professional Team Sport: A Refined Model and Empirical Assessment." *Journal of Sport Management* 22, no. 2, pp. 205–26.

bundesliga.com, 2018. "German Soccer Rules: 50+1 Explained." from https://bundesliga.com/en/news/Bundesliga/german-soccer-rules-50-1-fifty-plus-one-explained-466583.jsp

bbc.com, 2018. "Premier League TV Rights: Amazon to Show 20 Matches a Season from 2019-2022." from https://bbc.com/sport/football/44396151

Dawson, A. 2017. "The 15 Richest Billionaire Football Club Owners in England—and How they Made their Fortunes." from https://businessinsider.com/the-15-richest-billionaire-football-club-owners-in-england-2017-5?r=US&IR=T

Drazenovic, D., and M. Hizak. 2005. *Mogu ja i bolje: sportsko komuniciranje i marketinške aktivnosti u sportu.* Varazdin, TIVA Tiskara.

forbes.com, 2018. "The World's Highest-Paid Athletes." from https://forbes.com/athletes/list/#tab:overall

forbes.com, 2018. "How Much can the Esports Market Grow In 2018?" from https://forbes.com/sites/greatspeculations/2018/07/11/how-big-can-esports-grow-in-2018/#34fe6e866a36

Geigner, T. 2016. "The Perversion of Trademarks: Jose Mourinho Can't Coach Man-U Yet Because Former Club Trademarked His Name." from https://techdirt.com/articles/20160601/06114234591/perversion-trademarks-jose-mourinho-cant-coach-man-u-yet-because-former-club-trademarked-his-name.shtml

Gladden, J.M., D.C. Funk, S.R. Rosner, and K.L. Shropshire. 2004. *The Business of Sports.* Jones and Bartlett Publishers.

Gonzalez, R. 2018. "FIFA president Infantino Wants Big Changes to Transfer Rules Including End of January Transfer Window." from https://cbssports.com/soccer/news/what-to-know-about-the-transfer-market-changes-fifa-president-infantino-wants/

Groysberg, B., and A. Naik. 2016. "Is It Worth A Pay Cut To Work For A Great Manager (LikeCoach Bill Belichick)?" from https://forbes.com/sites/hbsworkingknowledge/2016/01/08/is-it-worth-a-pay-cut-to-work-for-a-great-manager-like-coach-bill-belichick/#7f9ca05d7d07

Havelka, N. 1992. "Socijalna percepcija." Zavod za udzbenike i nastavna sredstva.

Irish Mirror. 2018. "Manchester United Remain the No.1 Football Club in China, Beating Real Madrid into Second." from https://irishmirror.ie/sport/soccer/soccer-news/manchester-united-remain-no1-football-11952515

Kaplan, A.M., and M. Haenlein. 2010. "Users of the World, Unite! The Challenges and Opportunities of Social Media." *Business Horizons*. Elsevier.

Kotler, P., S. Saliba, and B. Wrenn. 1991. *Marketing Management Analysis, Planning, Implementation, and Control.* Prentice-Hall.

Kotler, P., G. Armstrong, V. Wong, and J. Saunders. 2008. *Principles of Marketing,* Fifth European Edition. Prentice Hall.

Maiocco, M. 2017. "Penalties have not Dampened Rashard Robinson's Self-Confidence." from https://nbcsports.com/bayarea/49ers/penalties-have-not-dampened-rashard-robinsons-self-confidence

Malovic, S., and G. Vilovic. 2005. *Osnove novinarstva.* Golden marketing-Tehnicka knjiga.

Mangold, W.G., and D.J. Faulds. 2009. *Social Media: The New Hybrid Element of the Promotion Mix.* Kelley School of Business, Indiana University.

Matheson, V., 2006. "Mega-Events: The Impact of the World's Largest Sporting Events on Local, Regional and National Economies." Economics Department Working Papers. Paper 68.

Molan, C., J. Matthews, and R. Arnold. 2016. "Leadership Off the Pitch: the Role of the Manager in Semi-Professional Football." *European Sport Management Quarterly* 16, no. 3, pp. 274–91.

Mullin, B.J., S. Hardy, and W.A. Sutton. 1999. *Sport Marketing, Human Kinetics.* Champaign, IL.

Nafziger, J.A. 2008. "A Comparison of the European and North American Models of Sports Organisation." *The International Sports Law Journal,* no. 3–4, pp. 100–09.

Ogbonna, E., and L.C. Harris. 2014. "Organizational Cultural Perpetuation: A Case Study of an English Premier League Football Club." *British Journal of Managament* 25, no. 4, pp. 667–86.

Pope, D.G., and Pope, J.C. 2009. "The Impact of College Sports Success on the Quantity and Quality of Student Applications. *Southern Economic Journal* 75, no. 3, pp. 750–80.

Ross, S.D., J.D. James, and P. Vargas. 2006. "Development of a Scale to Measure Team Brand Associations in Professional Sport." *Journal of Sport Management* 20, no. 2, pp. 260–79.

soccerex.com, 2018. "Red Card 2018—Report Released." https://soccerex.com/insight/articles/2018/red-card-2018-report-released

Srica, V. 1997. *Kako postati pun ideja: menedžeri i kreativnost.* MEP Consult.

Stier, W.F. 1993. *Alternate Career Paths in Physical Education: Sport Management.* Washington DC, ERIC Digest.

Sullivan, M. 2004. "Sport Marketing." In *The Business of Sport Management,* eds. J. Beech and S. Chadwick. Harlow: Pearson Education from www.eric.ed.gov:80/PDFS/ED362505.pdf

About the Author

Marijan Hizak is a longtime sportsman, marketing expert, and publicist. His life and professional career from the very start have been determined by sports. He started playing football in Croatia at a very young age and kept playing it until he graduated from the Faculty of Economics, University of Zagreb, and obtained his master's degree in marketing.

His professional career is also mostly tied to working in sports. Among others, he was the director of marketing of the Croatian professional football club Varteks FC (now Varazdin FC). Thanks to the Varteks FC taking part in the prestigious European soccer competitions, he had a a great opportunity to get to know the structure and organization of major European football clubs such as Aston Villa FC (UK), FC Mallorca (ESP), and SC Heerenveen (NL).

During his rich sports career, he worked with some of the most accomplished Croatian coaches, such as Zlatko Dalic (soccer), Zeljko Krajan (tennis), Branko Ivankovic (soccer), Miroslav Blazevic (soccer), and has been persuaded himself that along with the basic professional knowledge, professionalism and loyalty to work, effective communication, and personal promotion are extremely important elements of a demanding coaching profession.

Encouraged by the fact that a large number of sports coaches do not recognize the importance of marketing and communication skills, he began to deeply research and write about it. As a guest lecturer he delivered lectures on this topic at the Croatian Football Federation, Football Association of Slovenia, and Faculty of Kinesiology at the University of Zagreb. His first book titled *I Can Do It Better* was published in 2005 with a coauthor Darko Drazenovic, a Croatian sports journalist. In 2010 his second book titled *Why Are Some Coaches More Successful Than Others* was published in Croatia. In 2016 his third book, and the first one to be written in English *The Successful Coach – The Choice Is Yours Maxi!* was published. This is his fourth book—*Great Coaching and Your Bottom Line: How Good Coaching Leads to Superior Business Performance*—which is being published by the Business Expert Press from New York in 2019.

Index

OTHER TITLE IN OUR SPORTS AND ENTERTAINMENT MANAGEMENT AND MARKETING COLLECTION

Lynn Kahle, Editor

- *Artist Development Essentials: The Key to Structuring a Sustainable Profile in the Music Industry* by Hristo Penchev

OTHER FORTHCOMING TITLES IN THIS COLLECTION

- *Introduction to Sports Marketing: Marketing Through Sports* by Sanjeev Tripathi
- *Introduction to Sports Marketing: Marketing of Sports* by Sanjeev Tripathi
- *Marketing Movies Today: How Studios Are Leveraging Social Media to Promote Feature Films* by Karlin Reiter
- *I Pledge Allegiance to the Team: Implications of Fan Loyalty and Sports Rivalry* by Vassilis Dalakas

Announcing the Business Expert Press Digital Library

Concise e-books business students need for classroom and research

This book can also be purchased in an e-book collection by your library as

- a one-time purchase,
- that is owned forever,
- allows for simultaneous readers,
- has no restrictions on printing, and
- can be downloaded as PDFs from within the library community.

Our digital library collections are a great solution to beat the rising cost of textbooks. E-books can be loaded into their course management systems or onto students' e-book readers.
The **Business Expert Press** digital libraries are very affordable, with no obligation to buy in future years. For more information, please visit **www.businessexpertpress.com/librarians**. To set up a trial in the United States, please email **sales@businessexpertpress.com**.

www.ingramcontent.com/pod-product-compliance
Lightning Source LLC
Chambersburg PA
CBHW061331220326
41599CB00026B/5122